STAFF
COMMUNICATION
IN LIBRARIES

STAFF COMMUNICATION IN LIBRARIES

RICHARD EMERY
BA MSc(Econ) FLA
Social Sciences Librarian
University College, Cardiff

LINNET BOOKS & CLIVE BINGLEY

Library of Congress Cataloging in Publication Data

Emery, Richard.
  Staff communication in libraries.

  Bibliography: p.
  Includes index.
  1. Communication in library administration.
I. Title.
Z678.E4   658.4'5   74-23795
ISBN 0–208–01364–4

Z
678
E4

9/15/75 Eastern 9.90

FIRST PUBLISHED 1975
THIS EDITION SIMULTANEOUSLY PUBLISHED IN THE USA
BY LINNET BOOKS, AN IMPRINT OF SHOE STRING PRESS, INC,
995 SHERMAN AVENUE, HAMDEN, CONNECTICUT 06514
PRINTED IN GREAT BRITAIN
COPYRIGHT Ⓒ RICHARD EMERY 1975
ALL RIGHTS RESERVED

Contents

1*

TABLES AND DIAGRAMS

Preface

STAFF COMMUNICATION is an aspect of everyday activity which many librarians take for granted; they assume that their own particular communicative activities, and perhaps those within the library as a whole, are adequate and efficient. Staff communication, however, is not a secondary or derived aspect of management, but one that is central to organisational activity and is the basic process upon which other functions depend in their working and contributions to library goals. For this reason it is important that librarians appreciate the significance of staff communication and make a conscious effort to consider, evaluate and modify communication process and content. Furthermore, since staff communication itself, like many other aspects of administration and human behaviour, is a continuous process, subject to change and environmental influences, such effort should not be made simply on occasions when something goes wrong, but continuously.

Individual communication procedures should not be viewed or evaluated in isolation. Rather should they be seen as part of the total library staff communication process, which in turn should be integrated in the light of general theoretical considerations.

Theory presents the background through which any system can be initially understood. It postulates the relationships between elements in a system and gives indications for their current arrangement and implementation against meaningful considerations of purpose or goals. Hence theory promotes understanding of practice and a more realistic and rewarding enactment of such practices. For this reason due weight is given to theoretical considerations in this study. Practice in libraries is studied against a background of considerations relating to functions and ideals are emphasised in relation to specific forms of communication (*eg* staff handbooks) and the conscious initiation and development of a communication programme. The validity and inevitability of varying practice is certainly recognised but the importance of identifying common elements is stressed.

9

The word 'communication' comes from the latin 'communicationem' meaning 'making common' or 'imparting'. In communicating we are trying to establish a common meeting ground for understanding, for sharing facts, ideas and attitudes—for sharing meaning. Writing in 1963, L O Thayer reported that a survey of six years' communication literature revealed more than twenty five conceptually different referents for the term (Thayer, 1963 219). A common acknowledgement in definitions, however, seems to be that communication is a process rather than a static isolated object and that it includes all procedures by which people influence or affect one another.

Certain difficulties arise from such characteristics. Firstly, communication is a process which is open to change even as an investigator studies it. Secondly, the communicator faces the difficulty that words he uses are used in a given context and hence may be interpreted differently by individuals in different periods of time and situations. Thirdly, difficulties confronting investigator and communicator combine to present an additional challenge to the person who wishes to write or talk about communication. In the words of J A M Meerloo 'The attempt to communicate about communication is to be confronted at once with a peculiar epistemological paradox. The very subject we are to describe is used as a tool of description. By doing so, we are somehow continuously forced to stand in our own shadow' (Meerloo 131). Such a difficulty is, of course, scarcely open to resolution.

The present study examines the function and characteristics of staff communication in mainly public and academic libraries. Details of communication policies and procedures are based on information obtained from some seventy libraries in the United Kingdom, Ireland, the USA and Australia, plus printed sources relating to other libraries in these countries. Where relevant, information on communication in industry is also given. Since most of the information relating to libraries was obtained during the period 1971-73, some of the British public library names may now sound archaic in the light of 1974 local government reorganisation, and policies and procedures quoted in relation to individual libraries may now have changed. Such details, however, are presented as examples and therefore have validity as accounts of typical or exceptional practice of recent years.

The study is based on an FLA thesis presented in 1973. During the period of compilation of the thesis, numerous librarians were of assistance to me, providing information and opinion to facilitate my researches. In many cases their willingness to be of assistance went far beyond response occasioned by mere professional courtesy. In particular, I record my debt to Mr Wm R Maidment, Director, Camden Libraries; Miss L V Paulin, County Librarian, Hertfordshire County Library; Mr J A Howe, then Librarian, Luton Public Library; and Mr R J Bates, Librarian, University College, Cardiff, Library.

Some of the paragraphs used in the chapter on Informal Communication first appeared in an article, ' The library grapevine ', in the *Assistant librarian,* 64(1) Jan 1971 6-7, and are reproduced by kind permission of the editor of that periodical. Finally, I record my appreciation of the services provided by the interlibrary loan and photographic staff of University College, Cardiff, Library and the Library Association library staff. Their services considerably speeded the progress of my research and the presentation of both thesis and book.

R E
Cardiff
May 1974

CHAPTER ONE

Function

FUNCTION explains purposive action; that is function is usually thought of in terms of activity by which purposes are fulfilled. Not all sequences of behaviour lead to necessary or intended consequences, of course, but in general it may be said that functional activity should contribute to some wider goal or purpose. Viewed in this light, an element of communication (*eg* memorandum) should contribute to communication policy and communication as a complete concept, while communication policy in any one library should contribute to library goals. Communication policy thus embodies aims which are in themselves means to more general library goals.

H A Grace identifies four purposes of communication:
communication as utility
communication for communication's sake
communication for propaganda
communication for creativity (Grace 20).

Some of these purposes, especially that of propaganda, are more correctly applied to the field of mass communication. Elements of all four will, however, be present in the staff communication processes of any library organisation. Yet, since communication is not an end in itself, it is as useful to examine communication as a function, contributing to the achievement of library goals, as to examine the function of individual elements (*eg* staff meetings) of communication.

Since library goals differ, it is inevitable that communication and other elements of library activity (such as staff training), by which goals are to be achieved, will also differ. Purpose is something that man, individually or collectively, sets before himself as an ideal, an object to be attained. Discussion of library purposes usually indicates that the library is an instrument in society which should seek to assist in the best utilisation of existing resources and the enlightened development of the individual.

Library goals may be of a purely practical nature, such as the establishment of a service for housebound residents in a particular town, or may be intangible aims, those which may be said to place the library in its social context. Since the latter library goals are of a less determinate nature than, say, those of industry working on a profit motive, not only may diversification be great but assessment as to the progress a library or the library profession is making toward the attainment of its ideals can be difficult. It is possible to examine progress in so far as an increase in the number of volumes per head of population is concerned; similarly a more favourable ratio of staff to readers can be spoken of as progress. Yet it is certainly more difficult to say whether a public library is making an increased contribution to community education and well-being or a university library is further contributing to the volume and quality of scientific research by an increase in its stock.

The fact that purposes and progress toward them are not easily determined does not invalidate the value of purposes or aims, but it does cause difficulties in attempting to realistically assess elements such as communication, which are functioning toward the fulfilment of goals. As a result, statements of communication policy or assessments of communication in libraries are usually couched in general terms, being largely related to staff development and policy, rather than to wider library goals. The contribution of communication to satisfactory service, as well as to staff requirements such as morale, identified by Keyes D Metcalf in Harvard University Library (Metcalf 53), is not often recognised in printed statements.

Thus, points in Reading University Library's *Notes for staff* on channels of communication deal with the interrelationship of the work of the different departments of the library and established channels of lateral and vertical communication—in other words administrative and staff procedures and requirements. In notes to his staff on the importance of communication the librarian of Liverpool University Library is basically concerned with identifying the problem of communication between the librarian and his staff and between individual members of staff, that is the interchange of information and ideas, rather than the contribution of communication to general library goals (Varley).

The limited application of staff communication concepts in statement of policy is not, admittedly, a fault solely of libraries. Lynn A Townsend, President of Chrysler Corporation, in 1965 saw good

14

communication as a way of achieving corporate objectives (Townsend 208). The communications checklist of the Shell Oil Company, which lists fourteen major objectives (reproduced in Newcomb & Sammons 76), is, on the other hand, directed toward the employee, his information, efficiency and contentment, and does not relate communication as a function to company goals.

Library goals should, of course, include the development and well-being of all staff, such concern helping to provide a satisfactory relationship between the human and material structures present in most organisations and influencing the level of performance of staff with the materials at their disposal. However, to limit considerations of staff communication to the element ' staffing ' or ' staff control and development ' in the general administration of libraries is to place severe limitations on the significance of communication in libraries and other organisations. An examination of, for example, Henri Fayol's analysis of the six functions of management reveals that communication forms a vital part of all such aspects of management. The aspects identified by Fayol are: 1 forecasting, 2 planning, 3 commanding, 4 organising, 5 coordinating and 6 controlling (Fayol 6).

Forecasting involves the investigation of a situation, the study of written information, discussion with colleagues and the pronouncement of decisions. Such decisions relate to Fayol's second aspect, namely planning or the consideration of alternative forms of action, and the grouping of operations into homogeneous units for direction and control. Commanding involves the implementation of plans, the selection of one broad plan or one decision affecting a more limited field of activity from alternatives and the communication of such decisions to persons responsible for implementation. Organising, the provision and regulation of the necessary facilities both human and material, obviously involves ordering and obtaining such facilities and controlling them through communication. Coordination, the interrelation of work units and methods, is the concept to which communication is most obviously linked; it involves communicating decisions and information to all concerned and attempting to ensure throughout the action that each understands his or her part in the whole. Fayol's final concept, controlling, encompasses the activities of inspection to ensure that actions are taking place in line with commands, of eliminating misunderstanding and dealing with emergencies. It is thus directly concerned with explanation of directives and the receipt of feedback from people attempting to implement those directives. Thus communication is of vital importance in all aspects of management.

A similar organisational analysis, that of Likert, has been applied to libraries by Wheeler and Goldhor. For the purposes of evaluating a library's organisation the authors propose that the following points be considered:

1 the strength of staff loyalty

2 the degree of mutual confidence and teamwork among staff members, and with their heads

3 the extent to which each person knows just what he is to do and where he fits into the organisation

4 the extent to which delegation is effectively achieved and the extent to which staff members feel their ideas, knowledge and experience are being used in the library's processes of decision making

5 the degree of competence among various parts of the staff to help in solving library problems and the effectiveness of communication up and down and across the staff

6 the level of leadership skills of the department heads and their awareness of leadership processes

7 the extent to which readers are getting materials they want (Wheeler & Goldhor 183-4).

As with Fayol's points discussed above, it can be readily appreciated that communication affects each of these categorisations.

Barnard has gone so far as to maintain that in an exhaustive theory of organisation, communication would occupy a central place because the structure, extensiveness and scope of the organisation are almost entirely determined by communication techniques (Barnard 91). Similarly, J T Dorsey states that 'if administration is defined as a process consisting elementally of decisions, and if decisions are essentially communication phenomena, it follows that administration can be viewed as a communication process' (Dorsey 310).

These approaches to communication involve no real exaggeration of its importance. Communication is not a secondary or derived aspect of management but is central to organisational activity and is the basic process upon which other functions depend for their working and contributions to library goals. Communication is not merely something utilised by the senior librarian or administrator in his attempts to get things done. Certainly, communication plays an extremely important part in the work of administrators and supervisors. J S Morgan estimates that communication forms roughly 80 percent of the activities of such personnel (Morgan 10). Nevertheless, orders are ineffective unless understood and implemented and tasks cannot be properly fulfilled unless employees are given adequate information relevant to these tasks. Hence communication affects, and is utilised by, even the newest junior in the performance of library tasks.

Admittedly the value or importance of communication may be difficult to quantify in any practical sense. Usually improved communication is sensed by people working in the library or organisation concerned and is reflected in their greater satisfaction and increased contribution to library activities. Experiments have, however, been conducted in industry to measure the effect of improved communication. Gibbs and Brown in 1956 reported an example where considerable and reliable increase in production ensued when rapid and frequent knowledge of individual output was given to workers. This increase was due solely to the effects of information, as distinct from that of payment incentives and of propaganda in relation to some output target (Gibbs & Brown 374). Other experiments conducted into human behaviour suggest that restrictions of communication channels affects group performance by making it more difficult for the group members to organise themselves for efficient performance (Guetzkow & Simon). Such laboratory experiments tend to confirm investigations into real life situations, where work is not measurable in terms of production or output. Thus Pelz and Andrews reveal that contacts by scientists with colleagues stimulated performance through the exchange of information, ideas and enthusiasm (Pelz & Andrews 47).

Most works on personnel management or industrial psychology repeat the message in general terms, namely that employees tend to develop the will to do when they understand the work environment and its relation to their own individual interests. Not all library tasks can be viewed or judged in terms of ' production figures ' but, of course, the same considerations relating to efficiency and morale apply. Adequate information (and its perception) is necessary for the efficient performance of duties. In addition, adequate supervision of this performance is usually required and this supervision must be based on rational decision making. Hence communication is of vital significance for the working of any library in not only facilitating the solution of everyday problems but in aiding the formulation and implementation of long-range innovations. Most communicative activity is purposive activity (even though it may not be rational) and should contribute to the realisation of library purposes or goals if only through relation to more immediate purposes.

A library as a whole exists only to the extent that its parts are brought together in a network of internal relationships. Any organisation, in fact, is a means of overcoming individual weaknesses or limitations which restrict the individual seeking desired goals or ends. Organisations consist of people who, through cooperation, can achieve such goals. For cooperation to exist, a process of interaction and unification between people must be developed. Not all communication is directed towards agreement, of course, and group cooperation does not require that all the individuals must be able to communicate with each other. In the process of unification, however, communication plays an outstanding role and facilitates the direction of the library towards its goals. Although there are several connotations of the word 'function' (or 'functionalism'), its most important aspect is the emphasis upon systems of relationship and the integration of parts and sub-systems into a whole. To describe communication as a function thus helps to explain its importance and its contribution to library ends.

CHAPTER TWO

The process of communication

COMMUNICATION IS NOT successful unless the person from whom it issues achieves his expected purpose or results. Information or ideas do not themselves constitute communication. They can be issued by one person in isolation without ever reaching or affecting others and in such circumstances do not constitute communication, which is an activity conducted between people, not merely by individuals in isolation. ' He has a mania for written memos ' is a description applied to senior librarians in administrative positions which is quite often encountered. The inference is usually that many such memos are disregarded by receivers, due to their superficial contents or the sheer volume of their number.

The mere sending of a memorandum or giving an oral command only forms communication if it evokes a discriminatory response. Mere response to a stimulus does not justify the description ' communication '; response must be related to the intentions of the sender, providing intended results (successful communication) or disagreement. Thus E C Cherry defines communication not in terms of the response itself but the relationship set up by the transmission of stimuli and the evocation of response (Cherry 7).

Process

The notion of communication as a process, mentioned in chapter one, can be illustrated and appreciated from a consideration of the effects of communication. Simple models depicting the communicative act have figured in the literature of communication since the time of Shannon (Shannon & Weaver) and other writers concerned with the electrical transmission of information. Such models usually contain the following elements:

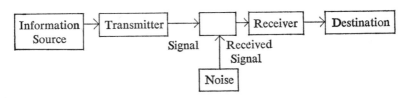

The process represented by the model involves a source selecting a message that is encoded into signals by a transmitter; a receiver decodes the signal so that the destination can recover the original message. The element of 'noise', interference or unwanted information, figured prominently in such models since the authors were concerned with the efficiency of transmission methods. The process is a linear one because it has a beginning and an end, a source and a destination. The messages that are received, however, also affect the messages that are sent in a communicative process. Subsequent writers therefore added further concepts to the basic model (*eg* that of feedback, introduced by Norbert Wiener) to create a circular process. An elaborated model can include the following elements and operations:

1	2	3	4	5	6
Sender's purpose	Sender's information	Encode	Transmit	Receive	Decode

7	8	9	10	11
Received message	Perceived intention	Receiver's reaction	Receiver's actions	Evaluation and feedback (return to 1)

Having established in his own mind his purposes for transmitting information, the sender must encode this or put it into the form of a message and transmit it via a channel (*ie* a means of communication, say, a written memo). Not all steps will necessarily appear in every communication attempt. There may, for example, be no provision for step 11 evaluation and feedback, although in such a case communication may prove to be ineffective in obtaining desired results.

'Feedback' is a term borrowed from electronics and information theory and describes the process which occurs when data regarding the performance of a system (*eg* a computer) is fed back into the system to permit correction and adjustment. The sender of a message is influenced, or should be so influenced, by the reactions his communication stimulates in the receiver, although reaction may not always be as explicit as in a speech dialogue. He may well modify future acts of communication on the basis of such experience or, in a situation of continuous communication involving the transmission of more than one piece of information (say in a conversation), adapt and modify his communication according to the response he is actually perceiving whilst so communicating. The communication model can therefore be drawn as a circle, or loop, with operation 11 leading on to 1, just as on a clock face the number 12 precedes that of 1. Acts of communication relevant to this model can hence be said to form a continuous process of reaction and adjustment.

The purpose and functions of communication have been discussed in chapter one. In everyday communication a person's purpose in initiating a communicative act or series of such acts will normally relate to more specific considerations than organisational goals. In initiating a regular series of staff meetings in his library a librarian may well be aiming at increased perception of, and progress towards, library goals as well as contributing factors such as staff morale. At a lower level of consideration, however, such as one item on a meeting's agenda or one order given orally in the course of a day's work, the librarian will be aiming at regulating behaviour according to some desired effect. In simplest terms, such regulation of behaviour can be viewed as the performance of a task (*eg* answering the telephone; relieving the reference librarian for his lunch break). More generally, the sender's purpose will be to : 1 modify an existing activity, 2 stop an activity, 3 start a new activity or 4 a combination of certain of these aims, such as stopping one activity and starting a new one (*eg* ceasing to issue books by the Browne method and starting to issue them by photocharging).

As well as having in mind certain actions resultant from the impact of his communication, the sender obviously also considers particular persons who are to perform these actions. Yet communication often produces response from persons to whom the communication was not directed. The sender may not have deliberately sought to exclude additional persons from the range of his communication for any such purpose as secrecy or discretion; it may simply be that he did not consider the content of the communication relevant to their work or interests. He can, however, often be mistaken in such assumptions and the receipt of part of a particular message by additional persons can lead to rumours, which in themselves may have a damaging effect on staff morale.

As will be seen in the chapter on informal communication, no librarian can foresee all the unintended consequences of his communicative actions but one possible safeguard, which will help minimise such disruptive consequences, is the open transmission and discussion of as much material as possible to all members of staff. If a library is particularly prone to unofficial group circulation or discussion of information, rumours or ill-informed resentment, the communication and morale positions may be improved almost at once by the introduction of certain minimum forms of regular communication such as a staff news sheet and staff meetings.

The actual effect of communication upon the receiver will depend upon: 1 his understanding of the message, 2 his perception of it—how he views it in relation to his own experiences, motivations, etc, and 3 his intention—what he intends to do about the message.

Understanding

A person may fail to understand a message because it contains inadequate information necessary for the performance of a particular task; the receiver cannot correct this deficiency merely by reinforcing his attention to the sender of the message, as he may well be unaware that the message is deficient. Thus a new junior member of a library staff, instructed to shelve books in the history sequence and to put all books on the shelves in order, could group books together by specific class numbers but ignore sub-arrangement by author within each grouping, unless the task was fully explained to the junior down to that level of detail. Inadequate performance of this duty could easily occur where symbols representing the authors' surnames did not form part of the classification notation and hence did not appear on the spines of books.

Alternatively, failure to understand a message may be due to simple lack of understanding of the message taken as a whole or certain words used in that message. Thus a library assistant instructed to put the fiction shelves in order may be given the following information: books are shelved alphabetically by author's surname; if the library has books by authors with the same surnames the alphabetical sequence of their first christian names is taken into account; if the library possesses more than one title by a particular author the works are sub-arranged alphabetically by the first words of the titles, omitting definite or indefinite articles; special forms by name, hyphenated surnames—arrange under the second part of the name, surnames with a prefix such as ' de ' or ' van '—count the prefix as part of the surname; treat all forms of ' Mac ' as one. The person so instructed could, however, arrange all books by authors whose names have the prefix ' Mac ' in a sequence before those with the prefix ' Mc ', not because the instructions have necessarily been inadequate, but simply because the task and problems involved are new to his experience, are unfamiliar and hence partly misunderstood. In a similar manner an assistant in a reference library, instructed by a more senior member of staff to answer an enquiry by looking in BUCOP or BHI, might be unfamiliar with these terms and the works the initials stand for. Hence the message could be incomprehensible.

In either of the above instances, where the whole message or certain words used as part of the message were not fully understood, resolution of the difficulty would necessitate further explanation on the part of the sender of the message. In the BUCOP example such explanation would be automatic upon the perception of the puzzled response to the first message (assuming it was not given in written form and opportunity for feedback was slight). In the case of the shelving of the ' Mac ' books, however, the task could be performed incorrectly (albeit correctly according to the junior's perception of the case) and explanation would follow only if the sender checked the junior's work, *ie* checked that his message had had its intended consequences. In either case it will be evident that adequate and effective communication is closely related to understanding by the sender of the possible defects in his message and sensible supervision of work.

Admittedly, it is easy for the senior librarian giving instructions to overestimate his listener's fund of knowledge and background information. Being familiar with a subject himself it is sometimes difficult for the supervisor to be accurately aware of how much information he needs to impart or to realise that he has omitted certain vital details. The receiver may not always help in such situations. Many listeners hate to admit that they lack information, due to reasons of pride or fear of appearing ignorant or stupid. Hence care and thought are required in issuing instructions on matters which are familiar to the sender but not the receiver.

Perception

A consideration of 'perception' helps to indicate that meaning is not inherent in words or language but is related to the physical world and human attitudes and associations. Ogden and Richards in their 'triangle' of meaning define 'meaning' as a relational term, that is a complex term made up of three elements: the symbol, the reference (thought) and the referent (thing out there in the world which is referred to; this term was coined by Ogden and Richards to designate the object in the physical environment to which the symbols referred, but always indirectly through the reference) (Ogden & Richards 11).

Dictionary definitions present merely crude approximations to the word meanings shared by individuals who communicate with each other about 'things'. If words, whose basic meaning is imprecise, are not reinforced by relations of action, quality and so on, relating to mutual experience of sender and receiver of messages, understanding may be lacking. Meaning cannot be transmitted as readily as mere words, since meaning or connotative meaning is a relationship between a sign, an object and a person, and is concerned with social as well as physical or formal reality.

Many difficulties encountered in industrial relations relate to imprecise definitions (eg 'cooling-off period') or the lack of reinforcement and explanation of such terms through the common experience of management and labour. In libraries, where all staff (save perhaps manual staff) share more of a common background and education than is the case in industry, such difficulties should be less but must still be borne in mind by the communicator.

A person's attitude towards messages, how he views and interprets them, is not a topic which can easily be explained or described. Likert has indicated that 'an individual's reaction to any situation is always a function not of the absolute character of the interaction but of his perception of it. It is how he sees things that count, not objective reality' (Likert, 1959 161). Perception in this context is, in fact, a function of a person's experience, needs and motivations. Shared background experience, mentioned above, aids the receiver to get the message as it is meant to be received and understood by the sender. It is unrealistic always to expect the sender to anticipate difficulties of understanding encountered by the receiver. The receiver also has to make an effort to take into account not only the bare informational content of the sender's message but also what he perceives to be the sender's intention (or lack of it), the situation and so on.

Perception encompasses considerations of the degree to which a person actually notices a message and how he views and interprets that message—his attitudes toward it. A message is often of greater importance or significance to the sender than it is to the receiver. At the time of communicating it is likely that the message is uppermost in the sender's thoughts. Furthermore, he may well have given a problem involved in the communication, and also his means of communicating (choice of words, written or spoken), considerable thought. Yet the message may strike no established thought pattern or basis of experience in the receiver. F C Bartlett has suggested that one of the chief functions of the mind, when it is active, is 'filling up gaps', that is constantly trying to link new material into the pattern of older material, in order to make it meaningful (Bartlett 121-4). Such a process is slow and often difficult, since our minds prefer the simple, regular and familiar to the complex, irregular or unfamiliar. Hence the value of attempting to assess the response to communication by supervision and observation of resulting actions and the reinforcement of messages by further additional or supportive communication. The reinforcement of orders or information initially conveyed orally by a written elaboration is an obvious example here.

Henry Heaney, Librarian of Queen's University, Belfast, has introduced a particularly useful method of recording and reinforcing decisions made by himself in oral consultation with his staff. Should any member of his staff (usually a senior member) consult him with the intention of eliciting a decision from him (*eg* on the type of library statistical records to be kept) the member of staff concerned is required later to submit a written version of his request and his interpretation of the decision arrived at orally. Such a record enables the receiver (in this case the librarian) to match the sender's advantage of prior thought and study of the problem, as well as affording him the opportunity of giving the case further thought when studying the sender's written version of request and decision.

An investigation by Ross A Webber leads to the conclusion that although any initiator tends to perceive more while the receiver perceives less, there are consistent differences in the perceptions of superiors and subordinates. The absolute discrepancy between the subordinate's and superior's perception of the superior's downward initiation is greater than the discrepancy between perceptions of the subordinate's upward initiation (Webber 239). Hence reinforcement of communication is particularly important in so far as downward communication is concerned (*ie* as opposed to upward communication of which Queen's University, Belfast, is an instance).

In any day-to-day work situation many communications are likely to lose their intended impact, thus not strictly speaking forming part of the 'communication' process, while many other completed circuits of the continuing process are likely to be soon forgotten, especially by the receiver. In an investigation into perceived interactions (*ie* communication which was perceived and hence subsequently remembered by the sender and receiver), T D Weinshall revealed that only in less than one half of all mutually perceived interactions did the 'recipient' of the communication understand the spirit in which it was meant to be delivered by the 'transmitter' of the communication. The communication did not 'pass' ('go through') in the spirit it was intended to go in 53 percent of the recorded mutually perceived interactions (Weinshall 625-6). Testings conducted by R G Nichols and L A Stevens into response and powers of assimilation indicate that two months after listening to a talk the average employee will remember only about 25 percent of what was said. Furthermore, after a person has barely learned something ' he tends to forget from one half to one third of it within eight hours ' (Nichols & Stevens 86). These considerations apply to intelligent as well as unintelligent persons.

It is obvious from the results of such research that the communicator needs to take active care in disseminating messages lest they are to be neglected in as casual a manner as that in which they are sent. Communication is related to habit and if it is desired to produce learning or changed attitudes in a receiver the sender must break some existing habit patterns and establish new ones. Undue repetition can, of course, lead to boredom and inattention, thus negating the sender's aims but certainly some repetition and reinforcement is necessary, especially when communicating new information or directions.

Besides tending to perceive what is expected or familiar more readily than what is unexpected or unfamiliar, individuals' perception of communication will vary according to their need for such communication. Thus an assistant librarian may well take more note of advice on how to reply to a request or complaint from a member of the public than, say, a memo instructing him to keep his desk tidy. In the former case he is seeking response to his own communication (*ie* his request for advice) in order to conclude an action (replying to a letter). In the latter case, besides arousing feelings of unbelief or hostility, the message was not sought by the receiver and may well be disregarded.

Closely related to considerations of need are those of volume of communication and relevance. A person receiving a great deal of communication will vary his response according to what he perceives to be the importance of individual messages and hence what may be an important communication in a sender's view may provoke little or no attention, let alone response, from a harassed receiver. Even interesting information tends to fade in a receiver's mind if it is unused by that person. Correspondingly, if a person has relatively limited communication with other members of staff (*eg* a branch librarian geographically separated from library staff other than his own branch staff), interaction with other staff (*eg* chief librarian or branch supervisor on the occasion of their visits to the branch) will appear more vivid to such a person. Hence such communication may have greater and more lasting impact on him than upon someone who communicates a great deal with many other staff (*eg* the chief librarian or branch supervisor in the present example).

It is difficult for a sender of messages to motivate an intended response since the receiver's response will in part depend on the latter's attitude to the sender and his previous communications, plus his attitude to the library and its purpose in general. A person's relationship with an object, event, idea or other person will play some part in determining the attention which he gives to it or to the other person. Thus people will tend to pay more attention to the unexpected or unusual than the familiar and will be differently ' tuned in ' to persons of different status. An assistant librarian will, for example, be receptive in different ways to his chief and fellow staff of comparable status. He may well pay more attention to the communications of his chief because they are more important, carry more authority, are less frequent and more unusual, than those of his fellow staff.

The mixture of a person's powers of reasoning and emotions,

all internal factors and senses which shape his views and actions, are termed a 'conceptual/evaluative system' by L O Thayer, indicating that an individual both conceives (*ie* comprehends) and evaluates an event, thing, idea, relationship, feeling and so on. Thayer indicates that this system is 'an extremely complex and intricately organised multidimensional hierarchy of concepts, values, beliefs, etc, and of clusters of concepts, values, beliefs, etc' (Thayer, 1968 43).

Such a statement adequately indicates the complex nervous system which determines a person's motivations. It may be possible to alter the relationship between an individual and his perceived environment (*eg* by counselling to make a member of staff more aware of the need to cooperate with his immediate superior). To motivate a person directly into adopting an orientation to himself or his work that is not at least latently understood and acceptable to him is, however, a much more complex task, possibly an impossible one. At a practical level, the most that the communicator can perhaps attempt is to try to provoke a rational response by a full and logical presentation of information; further than this a chief librarian or senior in an administrative or supervisory position can attempt to motivate intended response to individual acts of communication by maintaining general and consistent good staff relations and communication.

Intention

Even if a person receives a message that is structurally perfect and a perfect semantic accord (meaning) between sender and receiver is evident, the receiver may still take no action to enact the requirements specified by the sender (*ie* assuming the message is not simply ' to take no action ' on a particular matter). In such a situation we can still speak of ' communication ' as having taken place. The message has been received and understood, although no action ensues; hence the term ' negative communication ' is appropriate in such an instance. This fact will, however, be of slight satisfaction to the sender whose underlying purpose in the use of information has been thwarted.

As seen above, we tend to select sources of information with which we already agree. This is not necessarily a deliberate conscious choice to avoid seeing the other side of a question or to reinforce one's prejudices. Rather it is because the information from these sources tends to be understood more easily. Occasionally, however, an individual's attitudes can be deliberately obstructive. The decision of a receiver to take no action in such an instance may be due to his opinion that: 1 the course of action required by the sender is unnecessary, unjustified or misguided, 2 to simple lethargy and inertia, 3 positive decisions not to take action to annoy the sender or thwart his intentions or 4 lack of time or ability to pursue the course of action. In the latter case some fault can be attached to the sender for not perceiving such facts. In the first instance, that the action would be unnecessary, unjustified or misguided, the receiver's opinion may well have some logical or correct basis and feedback or response should stimulate the continuing process of further communication to resolve the difference of opinion. In the second instance the receiver is clearly at fault. With routine communication (*eg* a memo on staff punctuality) his obstruction may not be evident to the sender of the message. Should the communication be of a more important and individual nature (*eg* a direction from the chief librarian to the head of a department to commence a series of staff training exercises in his department) the obstruction will obviously come to light more easily and quickly and must be resolved by the sender.

A further cause of inaction may relate to a person's dissatisfaction with his position in a library and attempts to emphasise his own self-importance. Thus J M Jackson refers to a study of senior staff in a British engineering plant which led to the discovery of a process of 'status protection'. When these men received instructions from their superiors they often treated the items as merely information or advice. In this manner they, in effect, achieved a relative improvement in their own position in the authority structure by acting as if no one had the right to direct their activity (Jackson 166).

Improving Efficiency
In the above examples of obstruction it is obvious that communication is closely related to decision making and the other elements of organisational administration outlined in chapter one. The present chapter attempts to show how communication, as well as being closely related to the whole organisation and its administrative processes, is also closely connected to the whole person, his experience and knowledge, his attitudes and motivations. This may

29

be reassuring to someone seeking clues as to the importance of communication but it also increases the complications attached to the communicative process, the difficulties of transmitting meaningful and worthwhile messages, and hence the care and attention which should be paid to communication. Unfortunately such care and attention is often taken for granted by librarians as a self-generating and easy accomplishment, not requiring constant conscious and detailed thought and study.

The communicator, be he senior or junior, be he communicating in a downward, horizontal or upward direction, can take certain steps to improve the efficiency of his communicative processes. Besides preparing himself for communication, in the sense of collecting all the facts necessary for his messages and choosing the most appropriate medium (spoken—to an individual or group at a staff meeting; written—by memo, or via the staff news sheet, etc), the communicator must obviously make his message relevant to its recipient and to his own purpose in sending the message.

'Metacommunication' is a term used to describe any clue or evidence a person may use in slanting his message so as to ensure adequate reception. Such clues or evidence may relate to what other people are saying, how a particular situation is developing and so on. Hence it is evident that a communicator takes, or should take, into account more than the mere content of what is being said or written. The receiver of a message similarly takes into account more than the content of a message. As indicated above, he is affected by who is transmitting the message, that person's attitudes, expressions and so on. Thus metacommunication refers to the perception and actions of the receiver as well as sender, although in this section of chapter two it is the efficiency of the sender or initiating communicator which is under consideration.

Expectations are an important consideration in any communicative process. Expectations about each other's behaviour accompany any interaction between one person and another. In interpersonal behaviour we interpret our own behaviour in the context of what we assume to be the other person's interests, orientations, expectations, values and beliefs. In a communication situation the sender will adapt his messages and form of presentation to what he thinks will be the receiver's possible reaction and should hence always give due thought to the reception of his messages and the receiver's expectations regarding himself (*ie* the sender). Due thought and attention is needed to this aspect of communication since communication is usually an automatic process in the sense that the individual is not generally aware of considerations relating to source of motivation and expectation. Empathy, identifying with the other person, being able to see his point of view, understanding his needs, desires, feelings and expectations, is necessary for effective communication. Since all communication is persuasive, such understanding outlined above can readily facilitate the communication process.

'Noise', in the theoretical or electrical engineering sense, is often viewed as being a hindrance to communication. However, as E Berne has written 'In interpersonal communication " noise " is of more value than " information ", since in such cases it is of more value to the communicants to know about each other's states than to give " information " to each other. " Noise " carries latent communications from the communicant' (Berne 197). Hence noise can be regarded as feedback and also metacommunication, particularly from the sender's point of view. Such noise will not reduce intelligibly, as it would in a telephone system, but will form part of the communication process, will help shape content and facilitate understanding and rational reaction.

The human comprehending system (Thayer's comprehension/ evaluation system) has the advantage of being an adaptive one, responding to its environment, being influenced by it and influencing it in turn. In terms of staff the environment will consist partly of an administrative atmosphere or complex, containing decisions, orders and so on. Hence senior administrators, as communicators, have certain advantages on their side. A member of staff subjected to a particular administrative pattern or tone will usually become responsive and adaptive to it, hence aiding the process of communication. The proviso which needs to be stressed, of course, and has been indicated in this chapter, is that communicators should give due weight to the importance of form and means of communication, plus metacommunication, such as individual complexities, and feedback (or the individual's efforts at shaping his administrative environment).

The communicator who is aware of such factors affecting his efficiency is at least in the position of being able to attempt implementation of his theories in an effort to facilitate organisational efficiency and the provision of library services. Efficiency, of course, is not necessarily evidence of effectiveness. The efficiency of an action or process (immediate communication encounters) may be accepted as evidence of its effectiveness, whereas in fact it may be to the long range disadvantage of the staff and the library. Thus the imposition or restructuring of a system of library fines may be accomplished with great efficiency by counter, or circulation, staff. The results, however, may be to the disadvantage of senior staff morale in so far as the staff is particularly concerned with library service to the community and tends to oppose such charges and also to general library service in so far as it affects public attitudes to and use of the library. The resolution of such dilemmas can only be attempted by senior librarians viewing communication as a vital part of the administrative process and fully considering its function as contributing to the fulfilment of library goals. Some errors are bound to occur in communication but a recognition of the importance of communication in a library can help to reduce its deficiencies.

CHAPTER THREE

Organisational structure and communication

THE TERM ' organisation ' relates to a system by which departments and units are controlled and coordinated, resulting in an administrative structure, through which authority is delegated and control is exercised, and the performance of tasks (*eg* elements of library service). All libraries, in fact, have a formal system of administration, that is a set of rules regulating such matters as the division of labour, responsibility and power between members, the use of defined channels and procedures of communication, the selection, promotion, discharge and payment of staff. Parallel with this runs an informal system of behaviour and organisation, sometimes extending, sometimes modifying, the formal system.

The importance of organisation as a subject for study and control by the administrative librarian can be seen from a statement, issued by the Association of Research Libraries, in which the organisation of the library is seen as the ' librarian's primary management tool for focussing and directing the talents and energies of staff to deliver services to fulfil programme objectives. It is also a means of balancing and coordinating work effort and for channelling internal and external communications and relationships ' (ARL 31).

Two basic elements are implicitly contained in definitions of ' organisation ' presented in the above paragraphs. One is the basis of organisation, or departmentalisation—the division of work for production or service purposes. The other is the form of organisation which establishes lines of authority for supervision, in other words the structure of control mechanisms. Both elements require attention and analysis before relating them to considerations of communication.

33

Bases of organisation

Divisionalisation is a means of dividing up a library into small and flexible units so as to facilitate its administration and to accommodate peculiarities relating to stock (*eg* a large donated collection which has to be maintained as a separate unit). Admittedly, the ideal or logical method of division does not always prevail. Other factors affecting the departmentalisation of a library include size, ability of staff, accident and relation to other neighbouring libraries. The ways in which library stock and services have been divided up are, however, basically six in number:

1 function (acquisitions, lending, etc)
2 activity or process (orders, repairs, etc)
3 form of material (serials, rare books, etc)
4 clientele (adult, children, etc)
5 geography (branches, outlying sections)
6 subject.

It seems apparent that departmentalisation will continue to be the basis of organisation for libraries, although change is likely to alter the relative grouping and importance of the patterns of specialisation. Thus it is possible to envisage the grouping of subject departments with reader service sub-divisions to form a public service department, as is recommended for large public libraries by INTAMEL. The latter body lists library services under three general headings: administrative services, technical services and public services (Intamel 259). Such a listing could, of course, be applied to other types of libraries, such as academic and national libraries, where an important addition to 'public services' would be a research unit or research/information officer.

It is possible to argue the advantages of various bases of organisational division. Thus the arrangement recommended by INTAMEL might be said to provide better coordination of departments, reduce costs and allow the work of the three main divisions to proceed more smoothly than with an alternative form of arrangement. However, all libraries are unique in so far as they provide or develop organisational peculiarities and varying characteristics. Furthermore, various bases of organisation or combinations of divisions are probably most practically applicable to individual libraries, to accommodate local differences relating to stock, required services and available staff. Irrespective of the bases on which libraries are divided and subdivided, effective organisation and service requires not only a grouping that provides for homogeneity of one or more types but also a suitable form of administrative structure and the realistic and flexible utilisation of this structure in all forms of staff relations.

Form of organisation

The organisational division of stock and services, necessary for the manageable workings of a library, creates the problem of coordinating and controlling these activities or divisions so as to establish uniformities in service and the achievement of library goals. Out of the attempt to solve such problems of divisionalisation and integration develop the structure and formal relationships among persons of varying administrative levels. This administrative structure, relating to staff and positions and establishing lines of authority for supervision and control, can vary just as much as the bases of organisation or departmentalisation.

In relation to companies it is usual to identify four principal types of administrative structure:

1 *Line organisation*

This is basically a simple structure, a pyramid of several horizontal levels. Responsibility and control stem directly from general manager to superintendent to foreman to workers. Staff at each level report to supervisors at the next level above and each level of supervisors pass down instructions to the next level below. It is closely linked to the concept of central administration, which emphasises concentration of directive processes in the hands of very few people, and clearly defined patterns of activity. Such a form of organisation may be suitable for an organisation performing basically routine production functions but in an organisation, such as a library, employing numerous professional persons, it could stifle initiative and creativity, especially in the face of changes or unique emergency situations, involving as it does limited participation by most employees in the formulation of service goals and coordination of effort.

2 *Line and staff organisation*

As companies become larger they become more complex and top executives can no longer be responsible for such different functions as research, engineering, planning, distribution and other activities requiring training and experience. Accordingly, executives and supervisors retain authority and control over activities in their particular departments but this line function is aided by staff assistance from engineers, personnel officers and other specialists. This development has been witnessed in libraries. Division or department heads have in the past normally combined line duties with staff duties. The tendency in large libraries is to split off auxiliary staff functions and assign them to staff of a comparable or lesser status responsible directly to the chief librarian (possibly through the deputy). Examples relate to personnel officers; administrative assistants; supervisory office staff in charge of general accounting, supplies, salaries and so on (*eg* University of Michigan Library); and display or exhibitions assistants (*eg* Luton Public Library—responsible to the chief assistant). Such persons do not form part of the authority structure in the sense of being responsible for a number of other staff (except where, as in the case of the University of Michigan Library, he heads a department of his own), although of course they are themselves responsible to a person above them. Largely they assist the line executive in the performance of his function, their authority being an extension of their superior's.

3 *Functional organisation*

This structure is an extension of the line and staff organisation. More attention is given to specialised skills, mainly at the supervisory level. One foreman may serve as the production boss to meet quotas, another as inspector and a third may be responsible for maintenance. In libraries this type of organisation is sometimes known as ' service ' organisation and is usually linked to line and staff organisation. Thus in Britain many county libraries have county or area librarians responsible for services such as work with children and young people, music, and so on. A similar type of organisation exists in Camden Public Libraries where services include reference, bibliographical, music and children. The disadvantage of the functional system of organisation is that it mars the clear-cut lines of authority and responsibility of the line organisation, be they rigid or flexible. In the libraries referred to service staff intercede in the traditional pattern of librarian–deputy–branch superintendent/regional librarian–branch librarian, having responsibility for, say, music services in the branches as well as at hq. The advantage of such an organisation, of course, is that gains are made in terms of facilitating more specialised work performance and supervision.

4 *Group or committee organisation*

Some large companies, such as DuPont and General Motors, construct a network of committees to work with the line and staff organisation in order to facilitate communication involving decision making. A similar arrangement is evident in the academic administration of universities. Here committees or groups may be permanent and meet regularly or they may be organised to serve a temporary function only. This type of organisation has not generally been adopted by libraries, save in so far as it is possible to designate temporary working groups (*eg* Luton Public Libraries—service to teenagers) and regular staff meetings as this type of organisation.

As with bases of organisation, the form of organisation most prevalent in libraries is a combination of different elements, largely a combination of line (flexible) and staff plus elements of functional organisation. The latter combined form of organisation and any single form of organisation, such as group or committee, can be applied to any of the bases of organisation or departmentalisation, such as function or clientele, or a combined form of such bases. Thus it can be said that Luton Public Library exhibits the following organisational characteristics:

Base of organisation or departmentalisation—function, plus clientele, plus geography, plus subject.

Form of organisation—line and staff, plus group or committee.

Just as there is no right or best base of organisation for all libraries, so is there no right or best form of organisation to match a particular base. One evident tendency in libraries is for larger ones to adopt the more flexible and expansive bases and forms, namely function regrouped into technical services and reader services divisions, or subject, and line and staff combined with functional and group. In this limited sense it is possible to say that a combination appears to be correct, or the most advantageous organisation for large libraries employing numbers of professional staff, but to go further would necessitate introducing rather meaningless generalisations relating to organisation and libraries.

Similarly, it cannot be said that any one organisation (base plus form) is conducive to good staff communication and other elements of administration, although certain qualifications can be introduced to amend this statement. Thus the geographic base of organisation is probably less conducive to good staff communication than other bases. Due to physical separation of library units over a wide area,

37

communication between the individual units will most likely be less than communication between hq departments. This is not to say that library services in such a system will be less efficient than in a library with a functional organisational base, since much depends on the quality and enthusiasm of administrative staff, but certainly communication will be more difficult and hence perhaps less effective.

So far as form of organisation is concerned, it can be said that the line is efficient in terms of communication within certain limits. Such a system traditionally witnesses information going up the hierarchical structure and orders going down it. Rigidly organised, such communications would pass up and down in an efficient manner. However, the rigid line would stifle communication outside the formally accepted or specified limits and this could be disadvantageous to work involving creative thought and effort. Designed to be rational and logical, and to keep the human factor to a minimum, the rigid line organisation is liable to fail when faced with the irrational and emotional aspects of organisational life; designed to deal with the predictable, the routine, the typical, it is weak when confronted by the unforeseeable, the unusual and the illogical.

Many libraries and other professional organisations have a noticeable horizontal structure for communication and all administrative purposes. Hence it might be said that a line and staff form of organisation is more suited to libraries than is a rigid line form and that such a form is more conducive to general staff communication necessary in an organisation such as a library. There are elements of truth in this. But it would be much harder to differentiate between line and staff, functional and group forms or organisation, or various combinations of them, in terms of communication and administrative effectiveness. Similar considerations apply to judgements between bases of organisation (excluding geography) and to links between individual forms and bases.

Considering libraries in general, a more realistic statement relating to communication and organisational base and form would appear to be as follows:

Communications flourish and work most effectively in libraries with flexible forms of organisation, not handicapped by difficult bases of organisation such as geographic division, where the form of organisational or administrative structure is utilised through conscious effort by good administrative staff dealing with personnel arranged in reasonably sized groupings.

Since libraries are not generally organised for optimal communication but for other purposes or due to other forces, such as the desire to maintain an authority structure and the demands of specialisation and service, attention must obviously be paid to organisational base and form in any study of communication. The basic elements in the statement presented above will now be examined.

Flexible form of organisation

Some form of compromise is necessary between excessive rigidity, which can stifle creative communication and excessive flexibility, which can result in disorganisation and ineffective administrative efforts. Some authority and control structure is needed in any library or other type of organisation. Some system of formal structure is necessary in a library to provide direction of staff work, in the performance of library services, and general control during occasions of dispute or difficulty. Without some authority structure and rules work may be impeded due to lack of understanding relating to individual responsibilities and lack of directional control.

Such an authority structure does not necessarily stifle initiative or creative work. Indeed, some formal structure is necessary to encourage the display of initiative and direct and utilise its occurrence. Furthermore, since libraries employ non-professional as well as professional staff, a certain pyramidal structure is necessary to regulate such staff whose activities are not based on professional consultation but rather the issue and receipt of orders. Thus, to facilitate the work performance of varying groups in a library, the administrative structure, incorporating levels of authority and communication channels, should be designed so as to seek a balance between a too rigid and a too flexible system.

Flexible systems of communication must, as was indicated by Fayol (Fayol 34-5), be formal in the sense that they are provided for and recognised in statements or understandings of communication policy and practice. Two preconditions or prerequisites for intercommunication are 1 a relationship and 2 mutually understood rules and/or roles for enabling and regulating the transaction (Thayer, 1968 95). In a formal communication system such relationships and understood rules and/or roles should be administratively recognised and outlined, preferably in written statements, and not solely established and utilised by individuals according to their abilities and interests. This is not to argue that channels of communication should strictly adhere to lines of authority in a formal and rigid administrative structure but that departures from such adherence should be recognised by administrators and some effort made to define and approve the directions and degrees of departure from the basic lines of authority that are thought to be justified and reasonable. Hence the wider, more flexible, system of communication channels can still be thought of as adhering to lines of authority and responsibility in the administrative structure, even though not all links are shown on the library's basic organisation chart.

The process of communication involves the flow of material, information, perceptions and understanding between various parts and members of an organisation. The major channels of formal communication will be determined by the organisational structure of the library. If, however, communication channels depart too far from the organisational channels provided, authority and responsibility in the library may be impaired and certain persons with established positions in the formal structure may find themselves bypassed, thus reducing their information flows and possibly affecting their abilities to perform their jobs adequately. It is true that communication channels are in part deliberately planned, growing through usage, and in part develop in response to the social functions of communication. Formal communication, however, should not depart in undue degree from established channels. Provided that the structure of such channels does indeed develop through usage in a realistic manner for the needs of the library staff, this formal structure should prove adequate and not be subverted by spontaneous arrangements between groups of staff.

Good administrative staff

The subject of good senior staff, that is staff responsive to the requirements of the library, enthusiastic and cooperative, is more fully dealt with in a later chapter on aids and hindrances to communication. Here attention is drawn to the necessity of administrative staff possessing the ability to provide the library with a sound formal structure and to encourage the utilisation of communication channels by patient attention and example. An attitude of cooperation between library staff requires that each person have a sense of responsibility towards his work and that of the library in general. This in turn requires adequate levels of information and advice relating to functions and everyday tasks. To encourage each staff member to experience this feeling of awareness and responsibility obviously requires effort on the part of those whose jobs include the communication of information to groups of staff.

Continuous attention to communication, providing staff with examples of the administrator's interest in communication and related facets of personnel regulation and his own belief in communication, will help convince staff of that person's sincerity and the importance of communication. It can be disastrous to simply pay lip service to communication. Should staff become aware of this, it could have more damaging effects on attitudes and morale than the mere non-existence of communication channels or the non-utilisation of provided channels. Attention to communication can on occasions be reflected in an attitude of concern and demonstrations of opinion that all is not as it should be. This in turn will help focus staff attention on problems and indicate that communication and the library administrative structure to which it is linked is not perfect but a growing system, adaptable to new requirements and changing circumstances.

Other attitudes that are conducive to effective communication include a friendly disposition, an interested attitude displaying knowledge and concern with staff problems, a helpful attitude attempting to deal creatively with staff requests or difficulties, a questioning attitude that indicates a willingness to learn as well as direct and an approachable attitude making it easy for people to reach and communicate directly with the administrator.

Whether the chief librarian retains specific responsibilities in relation to staff selection, job discriptions, staff training and so on, or has delegated such areas of administrative activity to other senior staff, it is certain that his communicative pattern is likely to affect the communication pattern of the whole library, irrespective of the mere existence of channels of communication. Although he may have delegated prime responsibility for communication study and control to his deputy or personnel officer, it is probably true to say that his effect on the communication pattern will still be greater than that of any other person. This is because he is the head of the library hierarchy whose administrative structure and workings take form and directions from his office. In a large library, that is one with a staff of over one hundred, it is desirable for a senior member of the administrative staff, say, the chief assistant to have clearly identifiable personnel duties and that part of that person's stated responsibilities lie in the field of staff communication. Whether such an arrangement is or is not made, however, the attitudes and efforts of other senior staff, not the least the librarian, condition the effectiveness of communication.

Reasonably sized groupings
The question of personnel arrangement in reasonably sized groupings focuses attention on the number of people or links in a particular hierarchical level (say, the level of departmental heads) and on the numbers of persons in particular departments. The first aspect has already been touched on. Considerations of the span of control relate to the immediate command of an administrator or supervisor (*ie* the group of staff he makes immediately accountable to him) and the extended command (*ie* all the employees under his control —in the case of the chief librarian, all staff; in the case of, say, the head of technical services, all staff in the accessions, cataloguing, circulation and photographic departments).

The size of the immediate command is a more important consideration, size of the extended command usually being dependent upon the former. A restricted span of control inevitably produces excessive red tape for each contact between library members must be carried upward until a common superior is found. If the organisation is large this will involve carrying all such matters upward through several levels of officials for decision and then downward again in the form of orders and instructions. The alternative is to increase the number of persons who are under the command of each supervisor, so that the pyramid will come to a peak more rapidly, there being fewer intervening levels. This too can lead to difficulty, however, for if a superior or head of department is required to supervise too many employees his control over them is weakened.

The span of command is a relatively unimportant consideration in small libraries, even those employing up to fifty persons, since the services required (*eg* reference, children) will usually be instrumental in breaking up the staff into small groups under professional librarians responsible for the various staff groupings. Secondly, the span can vary from organisation to organisation. Thus in industry, where comparatively routine tasks are geared to mass production, spans larger than twenty are common and realistic. Libraries, geared to more creative and intellectual work and service, will correspondingly demand small spans. Thirdly, even if it is possible to enunciate ideal spans, the practicality of such sizes would be affected by the individuals in charge; individuals' knowledge and energies vary as well as their set duties and time available. Fourthly, a supervisor will find it more difficult to control a large number of departments or services performing different functions than a corresponding number performing similar functions. Thus a librarian might find it possible to supervise fifteen branch libraries whereas it would prove impossible to supervise such a number of hq departments with different functions.

Much discussion has surrounded the size of the span of control as related to industry (see McAnally 454-5). In 1943 E W and John McDiarmid reported the span of control in thirty two public libraries. In twenty seven of the thirty two libraries from fifteen to sixty four branches reported directly to the administrator (McDiarmid 105). In 1959 G E Gscheidle surveyed sixteen American public libraries and found most spans over fifteen (Gscheidle 440-1) and identified a trend of decreasing the span of control for top administrators through the creation of major divisions and/or coordinative positions under the direction of top level personnel.

The most prevalent span of control in libraries examined for this study ranges from six to ten. The span of thirteen professional heads reporting to the deputy at University College, Cardiff, Library seems an unusually high number. Luton Public Library has eight professional heads reporting to the deputy through the chief assistant and this number seems more typical. The trend toward decrease in America reported by G E Gscheidle has been mirrored in Britain. An example of this trend is to be seen in Nottingham Public Libraries. As part of a re-organisation programme begun in 1969, eighteen branch libraries have been divided into four groups on a topographical basis, each under the authority of a group librarian.

Optimum sizes of groups, persons working in a particular department under one head, vary according to the considerations given to span of control over supervisors at a particular hierarchical level. C I Barnard stipulated that the effective optimum size of a group should not be over fifteen; for many types of cooperation five or six persons is the practical limit (Barnard 106). In libraries similar figures apply as to the more general question of span of control. The number of persons working in each department of a library is often quite small. In University College, Cardiff, Library, for example, numbers range from one to six only. In Luton Public Library numbers range from one to eighteen. Two additional departments at Luton display higher numbers but are subject to particular considerations. The lending library has a staff of thirty nine, but sixteen of these are non-professional staff serving the circulation area and come under the immediate control of a circulation supervisor. The branch libraries department has forty four staff but here the staff is split between branch, mobile and hospital library sections, each with sectional heads.

The figures quoted in relation to span of control and groupings of staff in individual departments indicate that communications in libraries are not inhibited by large departments or unworkable extensions of command as is sometimes the case in industry. On the contrary, staff groupings appear to be geared to effective communication and this condition of effective communication may result if administrators direct their attention to forms of organisation, the communication channels which are closely linked to such forms and the actual performance of communication within the library.

Direction
The remaining sections of this chapter will be devoted to further description and analysis of the actual directions in which formal communication flows. If a library's distribution of staff authority and responsibility is not to be subverted, formal communication, relating to library work and less frequently library policy, should follow channels established in practice as being reasonable and consistent with library activities and authority distribution. The actual amount of communication flowing through such channels will depend on a number of factors.

Most communication, save an indeterminate amount of mass communication, is exchanged between persons grouped in relatively stable units. Applying this statement to staff communication, it can be said that much communication, motivated by work requirements, will take place within a department in which a person works, since the other people in the department are within easy physical access and purpose-related work activities. A qualifying factor, of course, is that we tend to communicate with people who are most likely to help us to satisfy our needs and that we may turn more readily to a friend or superior who displays a 'helpful attitude' than to someone who may be better qualified to help but who is personally less attractive and less cooperative.

Communication between departments will tend to be affected by similar considerations of physical distance, related activities and personal attitudes. Large departments, such as a cataloguing department, will tend to be self-sufficient so far as work is concerned and hence its staff will engage in less interdepartmental communication than members of smaller departments or sections. The flow and volume of communication implied in such a statement will, however, be modified by other factors such as geographic separation and personal feelings.

Direction : Down
The term 'down' should really be taken to imply 'downward and outward' because in most libraries there is a dimension of geographic separation between hq and branches or outlying departments, just as there is a hierarchical distance below staff at various administrative levels. The concept of orders passing down and information passing up the administrative structure, which is linked to rigid line systems, can be discounted in libraries. Administrative structures in libraries are usually more flexible, much more contact between staff and departments being in the form of professional consultation rather than the direct issuing of orders or transmission of information.

Communication directly stemming from the librarian deserves emphasis because of its volume and because he is top of the chain of communication links, setting the pattern for what occurs below him. Yet if they are to be of value to the library staff, in the sense of providing useful information and direction for the pursuit of library activities, the librarian's communications will obviously be related to upward communication. He must receive adequate information and impressions himself about physical resources and his staff's capabilities and progress. He may tend to communicate more with his deputy and senior administrative staff than the rest of the library staff, especially so far as oral communication is concerned. Nevertheless, he should attempt to keep in personal contact, say, through staff meetings, with all sections of his staff. In this manner he will, it is true, be communicating with groups rather than randomly chosen individuals but by employing such methods he is still coming into contact with individual members of his staff. A senior member of staff in one British university library remarked to the author that ' the librarian himself deals only with his deputy and sub-librarians, unless forced to come into contact with lesser mortals '. In a large system much responsibility for communication will be delegated to the deputy and senior staff but in such a case as that quoted, the librarian is obviously ignoring his own communication responsibilities.

Much responsibility for communication will be delegated to senior staff or heads of departments. They will, or should, be passing on to their own staff information and ideas passed to them by the librarian or other members of staff superior in rank to themselves. In this way they will be facilitating the downward flow of communication throughout the system, supplementing direct contacts that the librarian has with groups of staff or individuals at various levels. Sometimes the head of a department may merely be required to distribute duplicated memoranda or copies of a staff news sheet to his staff. On other occasions he will be reporting to them more directly, not only on matters of which he has been asked to inform his staff but also on library and departmental affairs which he thinks would interest his staff or be of particular use to them in their work. In Leeds City Libraries, for example, formal matters such as closing for public holidays and changes in internal routines and regulations are communicated to all staff by means of duplicated memoranda. So far as other matters are concerned, heads of departments and branch librarians are expected to keep their staff informed of interesting developments on a day-to-day basis. Such communication helps to inculcate a sense of participation in library service into all staff.

Downward communication can be scheduled regularly (*eg* staff meetings) or arise according to daily needs. The most usual types of contents are instructions to perform particular tasks and information (*eg* concerning staff changes). The sharing of opinions and ideas usually occurs within departments, between the librarian and senior staff or at staff meetings, rather than throughout the library structure as a whole starting from the librarian and reaching down to the junior staff. Finally, formal communication (*eg* the issuing of orders) is normally done through departmental heads, thus adhering to the authority structure of the library, or to groups of staff following consultation with the department or group head.

Direction : Horizontal
The literature on organisations has traditionally reflected a pre-occupation with vertical relations, problems of leadership, authority and control, and a relative neglect of horizontal or lateral relations. In libraries, however, horizontal relations are important since the form of administrative structure in professional organisations is far from being a rigid line hierarchy. In an organisation whose routine work on production functions is suited to a line structure, horizontal communication could be disadvantageous to the system. Routine situations for which there are standard work instructions and well-specified decision points could be disrupted by irrelevant stimuli, such as bits of information transmitted horizontally. Wilfred Brown argues that communication and decision making should be made at the ' cross over ' point between two units—the point at which one man has authority over both units—rather than below it. Otherwise people without sufficient grasp of the total situation and awareness of all the implications will be making decisions or will communicate incomplete and possibly misleading information (W B P Brown).

Such a system, however, would involve delay and a heavy load on vertical communication lines. In addition, it could stifle initiative and shared authority at lower levels. In situations where it is difficult to devise standardised instructions and decisions must be made by people close to the operation, regardless of their rank, horizontal communication is essential. Such situations occur in libraries in, for example, the answering of reference enquiries where certain procedures of method may be laid down but where initiative in, say, contacting other library departments or individuals for assistance, is to be encouraged.

The basic advantage of horizontal communication in a library situation is that it aids coordination of decision making and work among individuals and departments, horizontal communication taking place within a department or organisational unit and between these departments or units. Sometimes coordination in these areas is accomplished or enforced by a common superior (*eg* a reader services librarian coordinating and controlling lending, reference

47

and interlibrary loan departments) but often a library will rely upon the members of the related units to assume at least some responsibility for this coordination. Such a situation could arise where an administrative librarian or coordinator was alloted too many departments to supervise, *ie* his span of control was too large. Such is the case in University College, Cardiff, Library where much decision making is made by departmental heads and then reported to the deputy.

Administrative developments in libraries that have encouraged or necessitated an emphasis on horizontal, as opposed to vertical, communication include the development of subject departments, leading to a greater horizontal array of departments than a base developed around the technical services/reader services concept, and the appointment of staff (*ie* in the 'line and staff' sense) functionally employed. The person functionally employed (*eg* a display assistant or stock editor) could be responsible to a lending librarian or to the chief himself; there is in theory no clear or obvious line position for him. The appointment of such persons tends to extend the administrative framework horizontally and the type of work performed by such persons obviously involves contacts with numerous departments and individual members of staff. A person functionally employed may be designated administrative responsibilities and his primary function may even be that of communication itself. This type of position has not, however, been common in libraries as it has in industry, where the manager might be assisted by an information assistant, whose tasks are to gather data, issue reports, prepare directives, advise persons and similar communicative functions.

Apart from facilitating the coordination of work and decision making processes, the provision and utilisation of horizontal communication channels in a library has other positive and advantageous effects. It can help to overcome departmental differences or jealousies. This would be particularly advantageous where two or more departments perform related or similar overlapping functions, as for instance at Columbia University, Illinois University and a number of other United States university libraries, where units of the acquisitions department share in the cataloguing function, completely processing added volumes of continuations and serials and doing some simple cataloguing of non-serial works.

Initial disinterested or hostile attitudes between departments could, it is true, tend to perpetuate themselves because they lead to a breakdown of communication. On the other hand, frequent and extensive interaction, flexible interdepartmental contacts and organisational procedures tend to result in favourable attitudes in the working relationship. A work situation which requires extensive horizontal contacts, and an organisational structure that facilitates this, will tend indirectly to create positive attitudes of helpful cooperation. This can be of immediate benefit to individual departments cooperating with each other or to more extensive library cooperation, as may be involved in book selection procedures among all or many departmental heads.

Organisational structure is important. So far as horizontal contacts are concerned the structure should, where possible, incorporate clear-cut definitions of departmental responsibility so as to avoid unnecessary and time-consuming consultations and possibly the development of hostilities. Secondly, the channels of horizontal communication should be established and linked to the administrative structure between all departments. It may be as necessary to link departments with independent functions (*eg* lending library and reference library) as it is to link those with closely related or overlapping functions. The importance of these considerations was indicated by Joan Woodward who found that in industry, relationships between departments could be complicated by lack of any clear-cut definition of responsibilities, and independence of functions meant that end results did not depend on the establishment of a close relationship between the people responsible for particular departments: this situation tended to encourage sectional interests and exaggerate departmental loyalties (Woodward 137).

The facilities of horizontal communication channels will, of course, be used by individuals other than heads of departments. For example, an assistant in a branch library, required by his branch librarian to prepare a list of reference works suitable for addition to the branch's stock, could well consult the library's reference librarian, children's librarian or other staff in those departments without having to exercise such contacts through the branch librarian. Furthermore, many horizontal contacts will be between colleagues in the same or different departments. Such contacts will be occasioned by work requirements and colleague consultation, as opposed to consultation of more senior supervisors, and may be motivated by personal friendship or the desire to settle a problem, seemingly by oneself or on one's own initiative, without referring the difficulty upwards. These contacts will facilitate the completion of work and indirectly aid the individual's identification with general interdepartmental and library goals.

The content of horizontal communication includes a greater proportion of information, advice and ideas than does vertical communication, which is more preoccupied with instructions and decisions. Information might relate to details of a trainee leaving one department to go to another. Advice and ideas could relate to knowledge and impressions gained by one member of staff at an external course and passed on to some of his colleagues. Horizontal communication contains a good proportion of attitudes; in the case of this category it is obvious that the boundary line between formal communication and informal discussion is considerably blurred. In so far as horizontal communication contains orders these are usually phrased in terms of requests, such as a request to provide materials for a library display or to deal with a reader's enquiry.

It would seem to be a logical observation that the consultative nature of much horizontal communication takes place orally rather than in written form. This is so, but the volume of written horizontal communication certainly increases with the size and geographic dispersal of the library. Written communications in a horizontal direction are normally of a routine, somewhat non-urgent nature, such as the circulation of request or reservation lists or requirements. In large systems telex communications provide an important supplementary form of written communication between library units. These may relate to stock and reservations (*eg* Buckinghamshire County Library) or reference enquiries and information.

The timing and frequency of horizontal communications depends on the requirements of circumstances and individual personality. They may be occasioned by definite administrative arrangements, planned to facilitate departmental and individual cooperation and information awareness, or may simply arise through work situations. An example of communication provided by administrative arrangements may be seen in the Library of Trinity College, Dublin. Here a third copy of outgoing correspondence (*ie* non-routine, excluding for example overdue notices or query letters relating to book orders) on pink paper is filed and made available for consultation by all senior staff. These copies are referred to by the staff as 'the pinks'. They obviously provide a useful source of information on the decisions and activities of the chief librarian (thus forming part of downward communication), fellow departmental heads and other senior staff. A similar arrangement is in evidence at Bradford University Library where third copies of non-routine and non-confidential outgoing letters and memos are circulated to all senior staff.

More widespread examples of 'occasioned' communication relate to meetings of, say, departmental heads or senior staff in one department. Such meetings may be convened to arrive at decisions or formulate work programmes (*eg* forthcoming library displays and exhibitions) and consequently help to establish a sense of teamwork and diminish any status and personal differences among various jobs and their incumbent persons. Sometimes the meetings are convened simply to allow members to express opinions, not necessarily to arrive at any decision. Such meetings should have advantageous results relating to staff relationships and morale.

One noticeable element in horizontal contacts as outlined above is the preponderance of contact between senior, as opposed to junior, staff. This is because attention has been largely focused on interdepartmental communication as an aid to cooperation and coordination. Junior staff tend to perform work in one department, under the direction of one or more senior staff also in that department, and thus have less need to consult junior staff in other departments on formal library matters. This fact in no way diminishes the importance of horizontal communication. It is senior staff who set administrative patterns, encourage work performance and help establish staff morale. Hence their cooperation in the interests of library service, on a wider scale than that of the individual department, is valuable and should be encouraged.

Direction : Up
The flow of upward communication depends, as does the flow of downward and horizontal communication, upon the existence of opportunities for this kind of communication and encouragement to the staff to use such opportunities or channels that exist. The provision of opportunities and the encouragement of their use can be a time-consuming and difficult business for an administrative librarian. The librarian who finds that his 'open door policy' leads

to frequent interruption of his own activities by extrovert members of staff may conclude that such encouragement to his staff is unnecessary and set a pattern of library management in which considerations of administrative convenience dictate a reliance on centrally formulated policies and directives. Consultations with subordinates by the librarians in administrative positions may be viewed as irrelevant and perhaps even disruptive; hence emphasis is placed on the formulation and issue of orders.

Such an attitude is misguided, however, since it ignores the vital link between downward and upward communication. The formulation and issue of orders needs to be linked to considerations of the receipt and implementation of such orders. These considerations involve discussion and consultation with staff to iron out difficulties and offer explanations and the feedback of information relating to the success of actions taken in response to the directives. Furthermore, the formulation of orders itself, if these orders are to be framed realistically as fitting the library's resources and staff capabilities, should depend upon an adequate flow of upward information and impressions. Information from longserving subordinates as to local conditions and past experience can be invaluable; opinions from new staff can be refreshing and of equal worth. Thus the process of upward and downward communication is a continuous and linked process. Information flowing upward facilitates the formulation of orders; their issue downwards is in turn followed by upward data relating to the implementation of these orders; this data is taken into account in formulating further additional or supplementary orders.

The opportunities for upward communication are conditioned by organisational features and structures. John Brewer has remarked that the upward flow of communication is greater in units in which superiors' and subordinates' work roles are differentiated professionally rather than bureaucratically (Brewer 481). Such a statement has obvious relevance to libraries, comprising as they do professionally dominated organisations, in which many work relationships are of a consultative, as opposed to a directive, nature. Brewer goes on to say that ' The need for upward communication appears to be high only where there is a high differentiation of superior and subordinate roles which removes the superior from first hand contact with operating problems and close contact with his subordinates ' (Ibid 483). Such a view, however, evidences a somewhat narrow conception of 'upward communication' and appears to contradict his first statement. Upward communication should not be thought of solely in terms of information in the form of, say, written reports or oral interview statements, passing up a rigid hierarchical chain of authority levels. Equally important is less formal consultation between persons separated by one hierarchical level of status and between a departmental head and his staff. Both types of contact result in a volume of upward communication probably exceeding that of communication passing up formally from a low level to the top of the administrative hierarchy, since people feel more comfortable communicating with their equals or persons not too far removed from their own status level. This gives an indication of the fact that upward communication is conditioned by organisational structure as well as organisational features such as professional dominance.

Upward departmental communication is encouraged by sensible limitations in the size of departments relative to the work to be performed. A public lending librarian, for example, in charge of a reader services and circulation staff of more than twenty five persons may find his personal contacts with staff, especially with those working different shifts, rather infrequent. Furthermore, the value of staff consultation and upward communication tends to be lost unless the lending librarian delegates sectional authority as well as work responsibility to, say, a readers' adviser, interlibrary loans assistant and circulation supervisor.

Looking beyond individual departments, similar considerations apply to the administrative structure as a whole. Reasonable spans of control and adequate coordination of departmental activities aid the flow of upward communication by increasing time available for direct contact and consultations between relevant staff. The exploitation of such organisational features which facilitate upward communication will increase progressively once staff realise that their ideas and information are valued by their seniors. This in turn contributes to professional morale and to the function of communication in facilitating the provision of library services in the light of library goals.

A chief librarian or other senior member of staff could, of course, feel overburdened with routine communications. Such a situation was revealed by Millicent Abell in a study of a medium-sized American public library (Abell 95). It may well be necessary for the librarian to set limits to his contacts with staff. Thus he may stipulate he is available for consultation by staff on any matter during certain times. In general, however, the overburdening of a librarian by upward communications (as opposed to his over-burdening with work) is probably due to an unclear definition of his specific responsibilities and inadequate delegation of responsibility to his subordinate senior staff. Unless he makes it clear, for example, that personnel problems and records and matters relating to public relations are to be referred to his deputy, he will himself receive many communications relating to these matters. Such definition and delegation of responsibility have additional advantages which a general ' open door ' and ' open in-tray ' lacks. It encourages staff to direct their communications to the proper persons, through the proper channels and not by-pass their immediate supervisors. The latter situation is undesirable since it reduces the status of senior staff and makes their task of commanding the respect of their staff difficult.

Most libraries encourage staff to report or discuss problems with their immediate supervisor, while allowing the right of direct access to the librarian especially on personal matters. A *Notes for staff* booklet produced by Reading University Library seeks to make staff aware of lines of authority and communication:

' Channels of communication.

It is important that the staff should be aware of the interrelationship of the work of different departments of the library. The established lateral channels of communication between departments of the library and with other departments of the university should be used for the conduct of library business. The approval of the departmental head who may be concerned should be sought before varying these arrangements. Within the library the normal channel of communication is through the department head, but direct access to the deputy librarian or the librarian is available by arrangement with the librarian's secretary to all members of the library staff who wish to discuss career and other personal matters ' (item 15).

Staff at New York Public library are invited to discuss a considerable range of matters with their immediate supervisor, since often these are the most obvious and relevant persons, and such procedure does not weaken the authority of the supervisor as does by-passing them for higher officials. Such matters or problems, outlined in the *Handbook for new staff members,* include specific work problems, preparation for promotion, request for transfer, suggestions for developing public services or improving methods and techniques and so on (New York Public Library 17-18).

More flexible arrangements may exist in smaller systems with a heavy concentration of senior professional staff and hence fewer levels of authority to by-pass. Such a situation applies at Exeter University Library:

' While we respect the chain and order of authority, and certainly that of the librarian and deputy librarian, this is not hard and fast and in certain circumstances about certain matters we feel free to enjoy a more fluid approach. Any member of staff can come to see the librarian or deputy when either is free to discuss any matter. This principle we value though the individual may then be referred to the departmental head ' (Exeter University Library).

Even when staff are not required to first discuss a matter with a departmental head they usually will do so through considerations of relevance and convenience. Should a member of staff require direct access to the chief or deputy it is often advisable for him to make an appointment to do so through the librarian's secretary (*eg* Flintshire County Library). Many chief librarians and deputies prefer to arrange set times for staff consultations. This particularly applies to meetings with departmental or service heads. Archibald McLeish at the Library of Congress used to see divisional heads daily. The librarian of Bolton Public Library has an appointment to see each departmental head on the morning of each day. In the West Riding of Yorkshire the deputy librarian has fixed times for all fourteen principal officers. Such meetings present opportunities for both formal reporting and the raising of problems or more general departmental matters. Staff or group meetings are, of course, another instance of such fixed timing of meetings. New York Public Library has two staff committees, one for the circulation department and one for the reference department. These committees are composed of representatives from all grades or classes of service. Their main function is seen as acting as clearing houses for departmental suggestions and, jointly, for ideas relating to the library as a whole. Such arrangements have the advantage of scheduling the availability of the librarian or deputy at certain fixed times. Should such persons merely pursue a general ' open door ' policy their actual availability could be considerably less. As one county librarian realistically remarked to the author ' Like every other chief

I like to think that I pursue an 'open door' policy. In practice my door is seldom opened '.

One advantage of scheduled arrangements is that they provide opportunities for upward communication within established channels of communication, linked to channels of authority and responsibility. Methods of upward communication, such as attitude surveys and suggestion boxes, admittedly more widely used in industry than in libraries, may be viewed as detours of normal communication channels in the sense that they by-pass established lines of authority. Surveys of staff attitudes or opinions may be worthwhile if the librarian is seeking data on a particular matter and is concerned with improving a particular aspect of staff policy or library service, or instituting a new programme relating to such a factor. Such a survey, in the form of a staff questionnaire, could form part of a communication programme (see a later chapter on *A communication programme*). In 1966 Luton Public Library undertook, again by means of a questionnaire, a training needs survey, which resulted in improvements to the staff training programme and certain forms of communications such as the staff news sheet. Just before he took office in 1967 the librarian of Liverpool University Library, D H Varley, invited all senior members of the library staff to set down, in confidence, their ideas on how they would improve the existing organisation. Many useful suggestions were made and practical results included the inauguration of staff meetings and establishment of working parties, plus the institution of a staff news letter.

Used at all regularly, however, methods of promoting upward communication such as attitude surveys are in themselves indications of the inadequacies of the more normal channels of communication and their use should not be encouraged. Attitudes of staff may change over periods of time, thus presenting widely contrasting data, and frequent investigations of their attitudes may be disadvantageous rather than conducive to morale and work flows. They may be means of uncovering specific sources of irritation among staff, especially if replies to surveys are anonymous, but should not supersede everyday discussion with immediate supervisors or group meetings at which grievances may be aired. Irritations may be symptoms of a problem not the real cause, hence expression of grievances in written form with no provision for adequate discussion with members of staff concerned may lead to misinterpretation. Attitude surveys may be undertaken by interview and discussion, as alternative or supplementary means to written statements, but here again they are best related to specific problems or schedules so as to fit into established communication procedures.

Information relevant to areas of responsibility of other senior staff may be of interest to a librarian, as indeed will general information on the library culled from such sources as staff news sheets and library committee minutes. However, the data that he actually requests or requires from specific individuals, as opposed to that which interest him from various sources, should be related to matters on which he can make decisions. W J Reddin presents four criteria for assessing the usefulness and therefore the effectiveness of the data a manager receives:

1 relevance—on matters on which he can make a decision

2 timeliness—regular data should come at the right frequency, *eg* weekly or monthly

3 accuracy—to be useful, data need not be one hundred percent accurate but it should be accurate enough so that correct decisions are more likely to be made

4 presentation—managers should decide not only what data they want, but also how these data should be presented (Reddin 137-8).

While such considerations are most easily applied to regular written data (*eg* monthly departmental reports), the senior librarian should attempt to specify his requirements based on some such list of criteria. Such a specification will facilitate not only the accuracy and clear presentation of regular data but also the relevance of the irregular type of information passed to a supervisor by his subordinates. Awareness by subordinate staff of the supervisor's requirements in this manner will encourage them to pay attention to the relevance and clarity of presentation of their communications upwards. It will help overcome one main blockage of upward communication, which is that subordinates fail to transmit information simply because they cannot visualise accurately what information their supervisors need and require. Some upward communication will, of course, be irrelevant under any imposed conditions. Such communication may be of value, not necessarily to the receiver as a basis for his decision making, but to the sender, as a form of cartharsis or escape—release from tension and emotion.

Guidelines should, however, be established for the more normal everyday types of communication.

Reddin's first criteria, relevance, can be amplified under a consideration of the content of upward communication. If a department or a library is to function adequately certain types of data should be passing upwards to departmental heads and administrative staff. These types relate to:

1 matters in which the supervisor may be held accountable by those senior to himself. This really includes all basic accountability for performance of one's assigned job but may be more clearly indicated by highlighting an example, such as a junior's friction with a member of the public who may later approach the librarian directly with a complaint

2 matters of disagreement between staff in one department or between members of staff in different departments

3 matters needing a supervisor's aproval—such as the performance of a task in a different manner from the established one. Also recommendations for changes in, or variations from, established policies and practices in general

4 progress reports on work undertaken.

Such reporting may be used to measure individual efficiency and performance but in general exists primarily to help a librarian control immediate matters and improve the quality of his planning.

Most routine reporting is accomplished in written form. Most libraries require periodic written reports from departmental or sectional heads and branch librarians, if only to aid the librarian in the compilation of his annual report; plus reports on any irregular occurrences such as accidents and thefts. Bootle Public Library requires the submission of reports on accidents, damage, theft, vandalism, break-ins, public complaints and problems. In addition, each branch has an annual diary in which events are entered daily, this diary being inspected and signed by the director and deputy on the occasions of their visits. Sheffield's City Librarian requires the following written reports:

quarterly statistical reports from heads of departments
annual narrative reports from heads of departments
annual report on extension activities
annual report on the use of periodicals
quarterly report on children's libraries
annual report on staff from heads of departments

reports on staff when being transferred or resigning

reports on special occurrences (*eg* theft, accidents, complaints etc)

reports on developments recommended by staff, local and general.

Much of the communication relating to the categories of content listed under 1 to 4 above, however, is performed orally, this method being more conducive to day-to-day reporting, casual remarks and discussion. Millicent Abell in her survey of a medium-sized American public library reported that over 93 percent of the librarian's contacts with his staff were in face-to-face conversations. This may be a rather high figure to apply to all libraries and to all supervisory staff but certainly it may be said that at least 70 percent of a supervisor's contact with staff, and thus of upward communication, will be by word of mouth. It is important to emphasise that such figures relate to upward communication within one department or from departmental heads to the librarian and should not be taken to imply a large volume of upward communication. Most libraries witness few unsolicited comments of a formal nature passing in an upward direction between departments, save in response to requests or at arranged meetings. Most upward communication takes place on a day-to-day basis within individual departments or branches; its volume will vary and it will tend to merge with informal communication.

Whatever channels of upward communication are provided in a library and whatever encouragement is given to staff to use them, there will still remain a number of hindrances or deterrents to the flow of such communication. The individual may feel that, although information and opinions are welcome, no practical results ensue. Hence it is important that senior librarians accord due appreciation to information and opinions received and, where possible, display a use of information and implementation of ideas or, alternatively, an indication to the relevant member of staff as to why his suggestions are impracticable or his opinions unsound.

Information and opinions should always be received objectively with an attentive attitude and appropriate action taken on what is received. Pursuit of such policies should help to lessen a dilemma attached to the superior person in a work situation. On the one hand his decision-making responsibilities require that he be adequately and correctly informed by his subordinates. On the other hand his responsibility for evaluating the performance of subordinates creates the condition whereby he will most likely get less than adequate and correct information from his subordinates. Under such conditions the subordinate tends to tell his superior what the latter is interested in, does not disclose what he does not want to hear and covers up problems and mistakes which may reflect adversely on the subordinate. Such a situation is not conducive to good work relationships and work performance and may also create a distortion in the downward flow of communication, since in his efforts to maintain the status differences the superior is less than candid in his relationships with subordinates.

The individual may be personally deterred from communicating upward through fear of displaying ignorance or unsound views or through fear that if he displays enthusiasm his work load might be increased. Both these difficulties may in part be overcome by helpful attitudes and sound organisation. Administrative staff and departmental heads may seek to eliminate the first apprehension through adequate consultation and discussion with their staff. The second factor will probably remain in any library whatever the pattern of management set by the librarian. In part this is desirable since it may deter needless or unwarranted criticism and may help to quieten the more vocal members of staff. So far as the majority of staff are concerned, however, it is probably true to say that often a person's enthusiasm will be related to a desire to take on new responsibilities or workloads, hence these fears will not apply. Such communication upward may in fact be a substitute for a person's lack of advancement from a low status position to one of greater responsibility and authority.

This is not to deny that such fears do act as a deterrent to other members of staff. A survey of university libraries in the north east United States of America by K H Plate revealed that 80 percent of the middle managers (*ie* departmental and sectional heads) felt that they could only 'sometimes' or 'rarely' be frank with their supervisors in matters of library management. This attitude was explained in one of two ways: 1 certain 'problems' were not considered worthy of taking up the time and attention of superiors and 2 frankness was not always desirable when dealing with superiors in an organisational context. The middle managers were aware that organisational rewards accrue to those supervisors who 'don't make moves' (Plate 37). However, if such fears do act as a deterrent the position may be eased or overcome in part by adequate definition of job responsibilities and lines of authority. In such a situation a member of staff will know that his suggestions relating to matters outside his own present areas of work and responsibility will be channeled in the direction and to persons suitable and amenable to additional work. As a result, his motivations to participate in library work and decision making may well be enhanced and his personal professional growth and development aided.

In a sense, of course, rules, definitions of responsibility and tasks may discourage new suggestions or patterns of behaviour, not only because of the possibility of getting into trouble, but because they discourage the search for better ways of performing the same tasks and allocating responsibility. An ambiguously defined job may actually encourage people to look for new methods and clearer lines of responsibility; yet such a situation can also lead to uncertainty and unproductive effort. Rules are necessary and desirable provided that they are not inflexible and applied too rigidly. Such a consideration emphasises the main theme of this chapter, namely the close links between: 1 communication, staff capabilities and attitudes, and management style and 2 communication and organisational structure and administrative arrangements.

CHAPTER FOUR

Informal communication

ALL ORGANISATIONS have both formal and informal systems of communication or communication structures. Communication between individuals is a natural human activity. Hence informal communication is a perfectly natural phenomenon in a work situation and exists whatever the structure or adequacy of the formal communication system. Whereas formal communication arises from work relationships (*eg* heads of departments' relations with their staff), informal communication arises from the social relationships of people and is not controlled by library administrators. Yet the fact that informal communication arises from the ' social relationship ' of people should not be interpreted as being an indication that informal communication concerns only extra-work social activities. The informal communication system is closely related to the formal one, supplementing it in a number of ways, and affects work activities.

J S McCormack believes that since the informal system consists of social relationships, which may have the power to determine whether the authority transmitted through the formal system will be accepted, it is important that positions of authority in the formal system also occupy positions of authority in the informal system (McCormack 64). Yet such a relationship between positions of authority in formal and informal structures is theoretical and, furthermore, would rob the informal system of some of its values. Informal structures help modify formal systems and provide a source of adaptive flexibility in adjusting them to a practical working environment. Informal structures do not have to be formally approved and hence can be used to advantage in, say, by-passing figure heads and weak workers who fail to get things done in a satisfactory manner, or simply in cutting red tape by making exceptions to rules and policy that formal organisation could not sanction. Such occurrences would not be possible if formal and informal authority were closely linked as McCormack suggests. There is, of course, the danger, possibly in McCormack's mind when making his suggestion, that informal systems can disrupt formal ones or usurp their functions. This is why, before the days of Elton Mayo of the Harvard Business School and the investigations at the Hawthorn plant of Western Electric, informal groups were regarded as illegitimate, as abberrations stemming from some kind of division failure, and were to be stamped out by personnel activities such as training or rotation of personnel. It is not possible, of course, to guarantee that group goals and interests will be consistent with those of the formal organisation but, provided that the formal system is reasonably strong and geared to a changing working environment, the informal system normally provides additional facilities as opposed to disruptive alternative ones.

It is not necessarily true as suggested, for example, by Jane Forgotson that informal communication flourishes in the absence of official communications and withers when the latter improves (Forgotson). Keith Davis, investigating communication at a particular company, found that formal and informal communication systems tend to be jointly active or jointly inactive. Where formal communication was inactive, informal communication did not rush in to fill the void; instead there was simply a lack of communication. Similarly, where there was effective formal communication there was an effective system of informal communication (Davis, Sept-Oct 1953 45). Informal and formal communication may thus supplement each other and often formal communication is simply used to confirm or to expand what has already been communicated to staff informally.

Content

If it is not true that informal communication replaces a weak formal system, what does have validity is the statement that in the absence of good official communication the content of informal communication is likely to become more tenuous and more harmful to library morale and staff relations generally. Communication involves the transmission of information, opinions or attitudes between persons, the receiver responding to the transmission in a positive or disinterested, negative, way. In general, official communication contains more information, in the form of commands, policy statements and factual surveys, than opinion. Informal communication, in contrast, contains a considerable volume of opinion and attitudes.

The informal communication system does, admittedly, distribute information. The latter may be facts which have not yet been communicated officially. Alternatively, they may be facts which will not form part of the library's official communication, due to a librarian's ignorance of staff interest or needs for the facts concerned or to his conscious attempt to withhold the information. This may be due to its confidential nature or his knowledge that should the facts become known he will be involved in additional work or dispute with his staff. In respect of information the informal communication system may thus usefully keep senior staff, below the level of chief librarian, informed on important matters and can aid all administrative staff in their supervisory capacities by keeping them informed on what actions individual persons are taking. The informal communication system is even more useful as a transmitter of opinions, which stand less chance of being subsequently carried in formal communication.

In more general terms, the informal structure concerns itself with official matters under three main circumstances: 1 when formal information is incomplete, 2 when the information is ambiguous, 3 when incorrect information is given or when correct information reaches the wrong people at the wrong time. In such circumstances members of staff will tend to compensate for these deficiencies, to make their total volume of received information more meaningful and adequate in terms of tasks which they are required to perform. In her studies of industrial concerns Joan Woodward found that organisational objectives were frequently achieved through the informal rather than the formal organisation. A dysfunctional formal organisation could be compensated by informal relationships and this was particularly noticeable in relation to technical change, when a somewhat inflexible formal structure required supplementing. Such situations are witnessed in libraries where, for example, informal group discussions among staff often supplement less frequent formal discussions at staff meetings.

The informal organisation can thus make up for inadequacies in formal communication but the resulting informal communication may not always be valuable or efficient. Especially if staff are confused and unclear about what is happening and feel powerless to affect their own activities, irrational opinion may predominate over reasonable attitudes or facts as the main content of informal communication. The inadequacies of formal communication are likely to be heightened during periods of anxiety and change. These conditions may relate to the individual, subject to anxiety and change in his private life or his work position, or to groups of staff in face of situations such as local government reorganisation.

An important category of content in the field of informal communication relates to purely personal matters or extra-work social activities. Most librarians seem more conscious of this category of content, paying attention to staff guild activities, than to the content relating to work, often having an unfounded belief in the adequacy of their own formal communication systems.

In all libraries the direction, volume and content of informal communication is conditioned by personal attitudes and friendships, age and periods of service in the library, physical location of work, shift working separations and use of common rooms and canteens. Staff events or gatherings arranged by a staff guild or committee have the advantage that they bring together staff who might be geographically separated during working hours and encourage a greater volume of relaxed communication between staff of varying degrees of status or authority.

The librarian of one medium-sized public library, whose staff gathered together only once a year for a Christmas party, remarked to the author that it seemed to be a declining phenomenon to meet business friends socially; this decline was exhibited not only in lack of social gatherings but in a diminishing attendance, or request to attend, professional meetings. County systems in particular may have difficulties in attracting staff, scattered by considerable geographic distances, to social gatherings and, of course, much social and professional gathering may be initiated by organisations other than the library, such as a trade union or local branches of the Library Association. Such professional activity, added to geographic distribution of staff, led to the winding up of Surrey County Library's staff guild a few years ago and the failure to revive it, despite serious attempts to do so. In this county social events, such as Christmas parties, are limited to the district level, as opposed to the whole county.

The type of library and its clientele may regulate the type of social contact encountered by library staff. Thus in Durham

University, a collegiate university, there is considerable social contact outside working hours between library staff and academics and therefore less need for organised social functions for library staff alone, although a limited number of social gatherings for library staff do take place.

Small library systems often experience no expressed need for the establishment of staff guilds or committees, contact between the limited number of staff being friendly and quite informal even in a work context. Such libraries often limit general social gatherings to a Christmas party (*eg* Bury Public Library) or the occasional librarian's ' at home ' (*eg* Bradford and Southampton University Libraries). In the case of Exeter University Library the Christmas party is supplemented by an annual treasure hunt.

Staff guild organisations appear strongest in medium-sized public libraries where the unity of a comparatively compact staff has not led to the existence of too much anonymity between individual members. Dudley Public Library staff guild organises attractive programmes of outings and social events, ranging from river boat shuffles to beer and skittle evenings. So far as larger systems are concerned, staff guilds are strongest in libraries not subject to great geographic dispersal, although Birmingham Public Library's Staff Association was ' formed in 1937 to promote the well-being of the staff and to organise social events essential to the unity of a staff scattered throughout the city ' (Birmingham Public Libraries 15). It arranges social events and at its committee meetings discusses problems and difficulties reported by individual members. If justified such matters are then referred to the city librarian and if necessary to the libraries and museums committee. A recent achievement by this form of negotiation was the payment of bus fares for split duties (Ibid 16).

This type of activity embodies close links between the formal and informal systems of communication. Further examples of such links are witnessed when staff guilds arrange professionl meetings and/or issue a news sheet or magazine. As well as social gatherings, Luton Public Library's staff guild organises professional meetings, outside speakers being invited to address the staff on topics such as library school education and book selling. Staffordshire County Library periodically issues a staff guild news letter, which includes some features of a more formal staff news letter or sheet, containing as it does details of staff activities, staff news, appointments, promotions, etc, and any interesting developments in the library service in the county as a whole.

The link between formal and informal communication and meetings is sometimes embodied in specific statements of staff guild purpose. Thus Durham County Library's staff manual indicates that the purpose of the staff guild is ' to bring together the library staff socially and professionally and to further members' interests in, and knowledge of, the library profession in general and the Durham County Library service in particular ' (Durham County Library 16). The general value of a staff guild is that it helps foster a spirit of community among the members of staff, thus facilitating communication interaction both during staff guild meetings and during working hours. A staff guild which organises professional meetings is, in addition, helping to promote a common awareness of professional and local library problems and helping to stimulate discussion on these topics. This in turn encourages a serious informal communication content and the supplementation of the formal communication system.

Direction
Ideally, official communication is a responsibility of all staff, the lower levels communicating upwards to senior staff, either in response to downward communication or their own initiatives in relaying information necessary for the sound administration of the library. Yet for practical purposes an official communication system, especially in a large library, is likely to be mainly directed downward and horizontally. In the light of such facts the value of informal communication, of which there is likely to be more than one structure due to overlapping membership of informal groups, can be readily appreciated. Its direction is not officially determined and much of its meandering will be in a horizontal and upward direction, thus providing senior librarians with a valuable insight into their staff's opinions and feelings. Knowledge of such opinions and feelings provides a vital basis for correct decision making and planning. In addition, it can be said that informal links between staff in different departments and of different levels of authority provide valuable unifying links for the staff and the library as an organisation.

The direction of informal communication in a library can be investigated and depicted by sociometric analysis, which involves social elements and relationships between staff. Using sociometry, the attempt is made to identify informal groups, the members of an informal group and the patterns of interactions and relationships between these people. Sociometry was established by J L Moreno in his book *Who shall survive* (1934). It is most satisfactory for groups with defined boundaries, in which the individuals know each other at least by name and continue with some cohesion over a reasonable period of time. Such conditions apply to most libraries, which are thus suitable for the application of sociometric techniques. The latter consist in asking each individual in a group to state with whom among the members of the group he prefers to associate for specific activities or in particular situations. It is important to specify these precisely since the person(s) an individual prefers to associate with in a work situation may be quite different from those whom he would like as intimate companions or friends.

Sociometry asks with whom a person would like to associate, all associations being possible, whereas actual contacts are influenced by ' the exigencies of the situation, such as the amount of external control, area in which contacts are made, placement of equipment, conventions of the group and characteristics such as hesitancy, shyness or domination, that determine the actual contact ' (Northway 24). Yet the validity of choice measured against actual selection on identical criterion is remarkably high (Ibid) and is chosen so as to concentrate an individual's attention on preferred contacts and desirable aspects of these contacts. Hence the value of this type of study in depicting patterns of informal communication.

From the answers obtained the choices each individual receives are added to give him a sociometric score—in essence the number of times he has been chosen by other individuals as a preferred associate for certain activities, although no indication is given of the intensity of these relationships—and the choices made between or among particular individuals are recorded. The results may be depicted on a ' sociogram '. Such a sociometric analysis was undertaken by the author, at the end of 1971, as described below. The test was not a particularly detailed one, since this would have involved analysis of results in terms of intercorrelations and probabilities, sophistications not considered necessary for the present study.

Description of group. The four largest departments of a library, these departments having a total staff of twenty (including three part-time staff). Since, so far as formal communication is concerned, more communication often takes place within large departments than between these departments, the four departments were chosen not only so as to obtain a convenient grouping of twenty or so staff but also to demonstrate how informal communication crosses formal departmental divisions and barriers.

The twenty staff comprised nine senior and eleven junior non-professional staff. The range of ages and experience covered young juniors with only a few months' experience in this library and senior staff with many years of experience.

At the time of administering the test (over a week's period of time) there were no absentees from the normal working force of the four departments or changes in personnel.

Test. Questions asked were:

1 With whom would you most like to work in the library (disregarding in which of the four departments he or she actually works).

2 With whom would you most like to work with in the library, assuming that person remains in the department he or she is now in.

3 With whom would you most like to associate as a friend during and after working hours.

Participants were required to name only one person in each criteria (*ie* each question).

Form of administration. The reason for the investigation (that of research into informal staff communication) was explained orally to separate individuals. The three questions were then put orally to such individuals and replies noted on paper by the administrator.

From the record of choices made during the test a figurative summary sheet of scores is compiled. Each choice is scored as 1. Thus if a person ' i ' has chosen ' j ' on the first criteria or question a ' 1 ' is entered in the horizontal column beside i's name and in the vertical column under j's. If he has not chosen him on the second criteria a zero is entered and if he has chosen him on the third a ' 1 ' is entered. Thus the square under j's name and beside i's will read 101.

Each vertical column is added to show the number of choices each individual received on each criterion; these sums are entered in the column ' Totals—on each criterion '. These in turn are added together and entered in the column ' Totals—combined '. This is to indicate the number of times a person has been chosen—his social acceptance score, or choice status; hence that person's popularity under the criteria chosen for questioning, in relation to other people. (In the example given two people—'m' and 'n' have the most popular scores of seven each). A similar interpretation can be obtained from the figures in the 'Number chosen' column. This is obtained by counting the number of people who have chosen an individual. It is termed a person's social receptiveness score (in the example given several people share a score of three). Presentation of this information in diagrammatic form is facilitated by indicating a person's preferred companion. This is done by following the line opposite each individual's name and encircling the highest number(s) of choices given to any one person, provided this is a score of more than one. Reciprocated pairs ('friends') can be plotted by looking along the line opposite the name of a preferred companion. If his highest number of choices goes to the person who chose him most, the reciprocating relationship is indicated by putting an 'R' in both squares where their columns meet.

In common with other sociometric tests it may be noted that no one individual is chosen by every other member of the group and only a few individuals are not chosen by any member of the group. Thus the person popularly characterised as 'universally liked' is not found sociometrically and the person 'nobody cares about' is a relatively rare individual (Northway 34).

The target sociogram, as designed by M L Northway, is a convenient means of depicting the social structure of a group, the predominating relationships among these individuals, and the extent to which these relationships cut across sex and formal administrative differences or barriers. Four concentric circles are drawn, the areas of each division being equal to one quarter of the whole target. Each circle is used to represent the level of combined total scores, respectively 1-2, 3-4, 5-6, and 7-8. Persons are entered in the division corresponding to their combined total score. The target is divided into four quarters, radial lines being drawn from the centre of the circle to the circumferences. Each such quarter represents a particular department (A-D). Males are indicated by a small star, females by a circle. Seniors are represented by black stars or circles, juniors by shaded ones. Each individual is represented by a lower case letter (a-t). A line is drawn from a

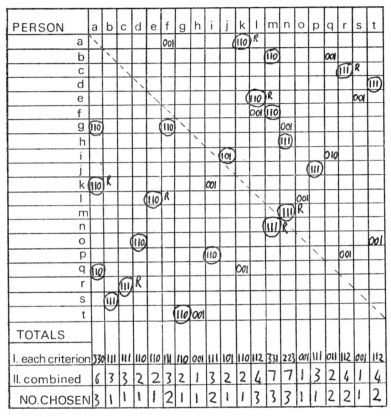

Fig 1 FIGURATIVE SUMMARY SHEET OF SOCIOMETRIC SCORES

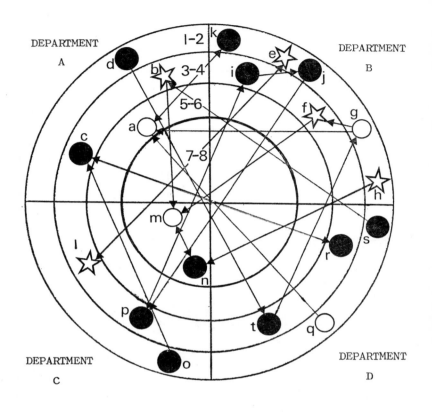

DEPARTMENT A

DEPARTMENT B

DEPARTMENT C

DEPARTMENT D

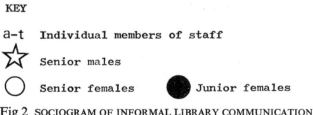

KEY

a-t Individual members of staff

☆ Senior males

○ Senior females   ● Junior females

Fig 2 SOCIOGRAM OF INFORMAL LIBRARY COMMUNICATION

person's name on the target to the name of the person he or she chooses most often and an arrow is placed at the end of the line. In the case of two people choosing each other more highly than they choose anyone else (reciprocated pairs or ' friends ') a double headed line indicates the reciprocal choice.

Of the total number of preferred choices (21, *ie* 19 persons with one choice each, and a twentieth person who displays two choices, having chosen two people with equal scores) only four are exercised in respect of a person currently working in the same department. This is not necessarily an indication of unsatisfactory relationships among persons in the existing departmental set up. Choices may be made based on an idealised conception of personal working relationships; in any case the test is designed to pin-point social relationships and friendships, not necessarily working compatibilities.

Sixteen of the twenty one choices are exercised between persons of the same sex. Too much should not be read into this particular analysis, however, since the group as a whole contains five males to fifteen females; a more even distribution of the sexes may have witnessed a more even pattern of inter-sex choice.

Of the nine seniors, six show a preferred relationship with another senior; three with a junior. Of the eleven juniors seven show a preferred relationship with another junior, four with a senior. Part of the explanation for this interpretation of the results is probably that two of the three questions related to association at work; hence for seniors at least common professional interests and capabilities, plus age differences with juniors, probably provide important motivations for the choices made.

What the results in general demonstrate is that informal relationships and communication tend to cut across departmental and status barriers or formal lines of division, thus providing a wider variety of staff links and association than formal authority relationships and communication channels. Hence it is possible to picture the interaction of formal and informal systems of communication and to appreciate the fact that informal communication, providing its content is sensible and serious, can supplement formal communication to the benefit of staff relationships and the library as a dynamic organisation.

The Grapevine

Some criticism of the grapevine—the colloquial name given the informal communication system due to its wandering course and hence resemblance to the natural object—arises because of its presumed fickleness and maliciousness. It is true that the grapevine is highly selective in its choice of material. This is partly due to the fact that, in contrast with official communication, the interest content of its material needs to be high for it to exist at all and because, being basically only an oral communication system, it is able to carry less material. Yet selectivity does not necessarily imply maliciousness or hostility, rather can it be interpreted to imply discrimination, exercised in terms of higher interest content.

The grapevine does carry rumour and personal animosity, even though the volume of this type of material is often exaggerated. John Garnett puts forward the view that ' The grapevine will pass facts accurately—and sometimes, as in the case of an appointment, before the decision has been made. But it always puts forward an uncharitable reason for the decision. The driving force behind communication is not " what " but " why ". The grapevine always passes the " why " in terms that are bad for co-operation ' (Garnett 9). This is a rather dogmatic assertion which is open to criticism. Keith Davis estimates that between 90 and 95 percent of grapevine information is correct (Davis, 1942 29). The percentage of material comprising false rumour and hostility cannot be eradicated and for particular individuals provides a useful means of releasing emotional tension through gossip and fantasy. The reasons for decisions may themselves comprise facts as well as opinion and the validity and accuracy of facts, and rationality of opinions, will of course vary.

If there is a danger in the grapevine it lies in the fact that, while rumour and hostility may help certain people psychologically, it can disturb many others. Also, it may lead to unwarranted personal influence within the library based primarily on social relationships but possibly affecting the library's authority and responsibility structure as well. Such influence is unwarranted because, while providing group interest, it can be detrimental to library morale as a whole, mitigating common effort for establishing or maintaining a good library service.

Grapevine information and opinion is usually distributed according to what Davis calls the ' cluster chain ' (Ibid 27-8), each person or link in the chain informing a cluster of people rather than only one person. Many of the receivers will not transmit the material further but may receive it passively or negatively. This means that the number of persons active on the grapevine can be comparatively small and hence arises the opportunity to develop personal influence.

Like the professional agitator, the library gossip monger will probably remain oblivious to rational argument should a senior librarian try to dissuade the person from spreading rumour or lies; such activity is, for the library gossip monger, part of his or her normal process of human intercourse. This activity is based on the person's psychological ' set ', which may include the elements of suspicion and hostility to all authority or influence, and is a necessary part of the individual's efforts to achieve satisfaction in social relationships and work.

What the senior librarian should try to do, as far as possible, is to remove the basis of the gossip monger's activity. This can be partly achieved by developing a good formal communication system, so that staff have less reason for feeling uneasy about what is going on and hence be less interested in rumour. This will not, of course, stop the circulation of all information or rumour. The grapevine is notoriously fast in the transmission of material and is quite likely to contain information which the librarian has not yet moulded into the form of a circular or speech.

Yet if staff are used to being officially informed of matters concerning their work and library policy, their expectations of receiving a particular piece of information will help minimise any fears or resentment they may feel on receiving it first from the grapevine. ' I heard it on the grapevine ' should not be a library lament bemoaning the fact that unpleasant or disturbing news was received from the wrong source and possibly not substantiated or contradicted from the right (official) one.

Rumours will develop even in a library possessing a good system of official communication, because not all rumours will contain material that is in process of being officially transmitted. What the librarian can do to prevent any bad effects of such rumour is to issue a denial or the necessary true facts immediately a rumour gets under way. If he maintains good official communicative activity he may hear of a problem before it gives birth to a troublesome rumour; alternatively, if he holds the loyalty of his staff, he will quite likely become a receiver on the grapevine and be in a better position to take quick action.

Two advantages are on the side of the senior librarian in attempting to counter any evil effects of the grapevine. Firstly, much grapevine material is ephemeral, requiring only time to lose its currency. Hence intermittent rumours will die out without harming library morale, provided the librarian does not neglect official communication. Secondly, the grapevine largely operates at a place of work rather than during out-of-work social contact. Hence the librarian has opportunity to study it and work on it, without seeing it slip out of his field of vision and action.

Occasionally administrators feed the grapevine information or ideas in an attempt to discover possible reaction to intended, or considered, action. This is a dangerous course which can rebound to the administrator's disadvantage, adversely affecting his plans and response to future official communication. What senior librarians can do is to consciously feed the grapevine correct information or reasonable ideas by practising the habit of chatting informally to their staff as individuals or groups. This can be done if it is desired to communicate orally in as short a period of time as possible. It can be done regularly merely to supplement official channels of communication and is often best achieved at groupings or meetings (*eg* coffee break in the communal staff room; staff guild social gatherings) which have not been arranged by the librarian. Official channels of communication will then not become cluttered with too much material and information transmitted through the grapevine may well be of more interest to staff and hence have greater effect.

Informal systems of communication cannot be eliminated. Rather their advantages should be recognised and an attempt made to mitigate their potential hazards. They are a permanent feature of any organisation and by helping to transmit information, by stimulating group loyalty and simply by their nature of oral systems which travel a good deal in an upward direction, are a valuable supplement to organisationally structured official communication.

CHAPTER FIVE

Ways and means

THE CONTENT and volume of material that a person decides to communicate should be related to his technical skills—his ability to communicate bare facts or detailed argument in a clear manner. This consideration must in turn be linked to the behavioural problem, to the audience for a particular piece or series of communicative contacts; the content and degree of technical accuracy which can be employed must obviously be related to anticipated receivers of the communication, to their knowledge, their feelings and attitudes.

Further considerations which affect the success of communication come within the problem area of representation, the means employed to convey information, ideas and opinions to library staff. Although it may be an exaggeration to claim, in McLuhan terms, that 'the medium is the message' (McLuhan Cht 1), the medium or means does exert an effect over and above that which is carried in the message itself. This may be related to source. Thus a librarian who always communicates in the form of written memos may produce a certain reaction from staff even before they have read his latest work. Or the effect may relate purely to the means of communication. Thus an individual may respond to information conveyed in writing, over and above normal reaction which could be expected from an examination of content alone, in a manner not repeated with spoken communication.

Since the means of communication is important, the communicator must pay attention to his choice of means—the decision whether to communicate in speech or in writing—and the expertise with which he employs his chosen means, in other words the general quality of his communication.

Choice
Choice of means should not be based purely on considerations of availability and ease of communication for the communicator. It

may, for example, be easier for the librarian to dictate a memo to his secretary, who is at hand for such purposes, and to have her arrange the distribution of such a piece of writing to all members of staff. This may be a lot easier than the librarian convening a staff meeting and having to discuss perhaps a difficult matter with a critical audience. Yet the latter method, the employment of spoken communication, may be much more effective in ensuring the fulfilment of the librarian's purpose.

Before choice is made the communicator should in fact give careful consideration to: 1 his purpose, 2 prevailing circumstances and 3 the content of communication. Only after careful consideration of these factors should he make the final decision as to means.

1 Purpose

Basic purposes are seven in number:
- a) inform
- b) convince
- c) reinforce
- d) rebuke
- e) request
- f) seek action
- g) counsel/advise.

Often these purposes are multiple; thus the purpose of communication enacted during a staff training session might be to provide information (to inform) as well as to correct previous performance standards (to rebuke). Purposes a) to e) are usually linked to f), the desire to promote action, although not necessarily since, for example, a librarian might distribute information relating to donations received via the staff news sheet. Such information would not be designed to promote action, except perhaps in the cataloguing department to deal with donations, although one would hope that the cataloguing department had been informed of the matter in a more direct manner, but simply to give staff in all departments a broader picture of what was happening in the library.

2 Circumstances

Purpose alone does not enable the communicator to accurately choose the correct means of communication. Obviously both oral and written communication can inform, can convince and so on. Such purposes must be qualified by prevailing circumstances, which may be grouped under five main headings:

a) importance—of the communication as perceived by the communicator. Short-term and long-term importance

b) time available—speed of implementation, of provoking action, might, for example, be desirable

c) level of communication and work—degree of complexity of the communication and the nature of the work or processes to which it refers

d) staff concerned—their knowledge, their temperament and likely reaction to the communication

e) size of library, administrative arrangement and physical location of staff to whom the communication is to be addressed.

As with purpose, the factors of circumstance may often be linked and apply in combination. Thus, even if a particular communication was not urgent and could be sent in writing, the presumed hostile reaction of the recipients might well dictate a choice of oral as opposed to written communication. Hence it may be seen that if the factors of circumstance are taken into account the choice of means will become more obvious. Thus, relating the variables of circumstance to those of purpose, if the communicator desires to inform an individual member of staff as quickly as possible it would seem logical to choose oral means of communication, employing face-to-face communication if the member of staff was within summoning distance or the telephone if geographic distance interposed.

3 Content

Before the final choice of means is made, consideration must be given to the content of communication. Content may basically comprise:

a) information
b) orders
c) ideas
d) opinions.

Information communicated in a library typically comprises personal information dealing with the individual's place in the library and his responsibilities; operational information concerned with his job; and background information describing the individual's wider working environment and dealing with such things as library goals and the functions and work of other departments.

All libraries endeavour to get work done and to enforce certain standards of work performance. Hence orders are a necessary complement to information. Most employees realise that they are obliged to accept certain kinds of orders from supervisors to do certain things. Such orders might be viewed as constraining the individual's freedom to exercise his own judgement, but are necessary to counteract the effects of immature or inexperienced judgements and to enforce library policies. Even so, orders should be realistic, that is capable of being enacted by the individual concerned, should give sufficient reasons and background information to promote understanding and compliance and facilitate enactment. Finally, in a professional organisation orders should where possible leave room for responsible and reasonable levels of discretion.

Etzioni distinguishes between two categories of organisational communication, namely instrumental communications and expressive communications (Etzioni, 1961 138). Information and orders fall into his first category, of instrumental communications. These are designed to affect individuals' perceptions relating to their work and to effect action. Expressive communications include the third and fourth categories of content listed above, namely ideas and opinions, being designed to facilitate the gradual formation, reinforcement and possible change of staff attitudes, and hence indirectly their work. Although neglected in many libraries, expressive communication is extremely important in helping to present staff with a wider picture of their working environment, its policies and justifications, than may be obtained from information and orders alone. It reinforces information and orders and, since it is aimed at staff attitudes, is helpful from the motivational point of view.

The types of content enumerated above are related to the variables of purpose and circumstance. Thus the issuance of orders will be affected by factors such as the physical location of staff and the purpose such as the need to effect action. The variables of purpose, circumstance and content should not, however, be related to each other in any very precise or dogmatic fashion. The advocacy of written communication for facts and spoken communication for reasons (Irving 13) may be sound general advice but is unrelated to variables of circumstance. Thus, if time available is limited it may prove necessary to communicate facts and reasons in spoken form; if a matter is particularly complicated it might prove more satisfactory to present a complete case of facts and reasons in written form.

General trends relating to communication are visible in libraries. Thus, as indicated below, the larger the system and hence the greater the physical distribution of staff and their separation in the organisational structure, the more the perceived need to communicate information and orders in written form. Yet a generalisation of this type is, of course, always conditioned by variables of circumstance, such as importance or time available. Hence the three categories of variable—purpose, circumstance and content—should always be generally related to each other. If the librarian analyses his need to communicate in the light of such variables, his decision as to the means employed should be that much more rational. This is not to suggest that communication is always the result of planned deliberation and choice but if the communicator is aware of the variables involved they will form a part of his unconscious decision processes.

The choice of means will not always be clear-cut in the sense that either spoken or written communication is chosen to the exclusion of the other. Often a combination of both types is desirable or helpful in situations, say, where it is desired to ' carry home ' ideas or a message. It is often extremely useful and effective to follow up, or reinforce, spoken with written communication. The broad outline of a proposed course of action might be presented orally to staff with clarity and the opportunity taken to overcome resentment and enter into discussion; more details might be circulated in written form. Such written reinforcement is also valuable where a permanent record of facts and decisions is necessary, perhaps as part of a staff manual or file of administrative memoranda.

Even if the choice of means appears to be clear-cut, it may prove effective to take a deliberately and seemingly irrational or illogical choice, favouring the alternative means. This is sometimes useful in circumstances where a means or form of communication has become stereotyped. If the latter is the case, the communication is liable to be judged by recipients in terms of the kind of information or material usually contained in similar types of communication; hence a lot of its impact will be lost, a lot of its content virtually ignored. Thus the librarian might occasionally find it useful to communicate orally at one or more staff meetings (depending on the size of the establishment) the type of routine information normally contained in staff news sheets or memos. Such a move could lead to renewed staff interest and might provoke useful discussion on related topics.

Expertise

Whatever means or combination of means is chosen by the communicator, the effect of the communication will depend not only on factors such as staff attitudes but also on the quality of the communication. A communicator may lose advantages relating to awareness of variables and employment of correct means if the means is then poorly employed or utilised.

In utilising a given means of communication, be it spoken or written, attention should be paid to arrangement of material and choice of words. Logical and helpful arrangement of material and arguments as well as sentences facilitate understanding; clear structure helps the receiver to predict what is coming, on the basis of what has passed, and thus reduces uncertainty and confusion. In English, redundancy is about 50 percent; that is, about half of the letters or words we choose in writing or speaking are under our free choice; about half are really controlled by the structure of the language. It is to the 50 percent under the communicator's choice that these comments about clear and logical arrangement or structure apply.

Psychologists vary in their opinions as to whether the important key part of a communication should appear at the beginning or the end, although they agree that the middle is the greatest area of superficial receiver attention and therefore to be avoided so far as important content is concerned. Especially if the spoken word is involved, however, the position may be varied according to the receptive nature of the audience. Where interest is high it seems advisable to save the key points for last, since interest may fade if the important elements of a communication are dispatched at the beginning. If, however, interest is low it may be possible to motivate arousal or interest by opening with key points.

Considering the choice of words, M Argyle maintains that 'words differ from other physical stimuli in that they have agreed meanings' (Argyle 64). Yet words as symbols designating objects or feelings mean different things to different people at different times and places, because of their different levels of understanding, different viewpoints and backgrounds. Argyle's statement is only true if emphasis is placed on denotive (*ie* dictionary definition) meaning. When connative (*ie* use in particular circumstances) meaning is emphasised it is obvious that other people's meanings may well be slightly different from one's own. Hence the need for careful choice of words relating to particular circumstances. For similar reasons the manner of presentation (*eg* logical or emotional) requires careful consideration. An emotional appeal to staff may work well in certain circumstances but if applied incorrectly or repeated too often could have a negative effect.

Such directives may be applied to both spoken and written forms of communication. Obviously the success of their application, the success of the whole communication process, in good measure relates to the ability of the individual involved to state his ideas or information simply and effectively, that is quality of material and means is conditioned by the quality of the human manipulator. Bearing in mind the importance of qualifying factors, that is of the relationship between the variables of purpose, circumstance and content, the general prevailing positions relating to staff communication in libraries will now be examined under the headings of spoken and written communication.

Spoken communication
Speech has certain general advantages over written communication, provided that circumstances and human deficiencies are not grossly unusual or exaggerated. The speaker has greater flexibility, in the sense that he can manipulate language. He does not necessarily have to speak in sentences, he can produce shades of meaning by stressing one word rather than another, in a group of words or sentence and can emphasise importance by use of repetition. In addition, the speaker has instant feedback, can see certain effects of what he is saying on the receiver and can modify or clarify his communication as necessary.

In contrast with written communication or spoken communication to groups, it is not always possible for the person communicating to individuals in everyday work situations to prepare in advance for speech or conversation; oral discourse is typically demanded for situations that are only generally and perhaps vaguely forseeable. A speaker must therefore develop a generalised ability to communicate clearly on what he knows or thinks about a wide variety of topics relating to his work in a variety of circumstances (Oliver 267).

a) Spoken communication to individuals

The communication act itself covers the stages or processes of the approach to contact with another person, the contact itself and the ending of communication. Numerous guides to communication and business management exist which offer sound advice on the processes, the techniques to be employed and so on (eg BACIE 1960). Such advice, however, is usually directed at the manager or supervisor who is communicating down to his staff. It is just as necessary to pay attention to the technique of listening. All supervisors should attempt to encourage and stimulate feedback and upward communication by sympathetic attention, since this type of communication is a complement to their own downward form.

Listening is a positive performance. Thought processes are four to five times the usual speed of speech and hence it is quite normal for a listener's attention to wander, for him to become bored or for him to interrupt the speaker before the latter has finished. Such tendencies should be consciously avoided; the listener should concentrate, adopt a positive frame of mind and if necessary assist the speaker with comment and a review of the subject or discussion once the speaker has had sufficient opportunity to state his case. This type of listening and response helps the speaker to perform at a higher level, showing him that the receiver is interested and motivating the speaker to do better.

In all types and sizes of libraries spoken communication tends to predominate over written communication so far as horizontal communication is concerned, especially that between individuals working in the same department. A similar trend is visible in upward communication. The upward transmission of information and ideas or complaints, often communicated in the form of discussion, uses the spoken means, the written means being reserved for routine reports such as monthly issue figures.

The most important factor affecting choice of means for downward communication in libraries is size and structure of the library; this appears to be of greater significance than any variable of purpose or content. Small libraries favour use of speech in downward communication. Thus Brunel University Library with a staff of 28 (Feb 1972) employs no staff news sheet and few memos in its communication. Staff get to know of important developments, such as the appointment of new staff, by being directly informed by the librarian or deputy. Written directives or instructions are limited to routine matters (*eg* holiday arrangements) or permanent directives (often discussed first; the written directive supplements the spoken discussion and provides a permanent record of decisions) which apply to all or the majority of staff. Similar use of communication is employed in Bury Public Library with a staff of 23 (March 1972).

The larger the system and the greater the physical distribution of staff and their separation in the organisational structure, the more the perceived need to communicate orders and information in written form. Within individual departments oral communication will still tend to predominate but convenience and necessity dictate a greater volume of written communication in a large or even medium-sized system with a staff of, say, 80 to 150. This trend in favour of written communication applies even if most staff are located in one building and not scattered geographically. Somewhat paradoxically, one result of this is that in such systems ideas and attitudes, as opposed to information and orders, predominate in oral downward communication.

This is no guarantee, however, that the volume of ideas and attitudes communicated will be as great as the volume of information and ideas communicated orally in a smaller system. Unfortunately, the larger system often witnesses an over-concentration on the communication of information and orders and hence on written communication. Written communication is easier under certain circumstances. It is easier to rebuke a person in writing than face-to-face; a suggestion can be turned down in a letter or memo without giving the proposer chance for a comeback, refinement or modification of his ideas; unpopular decisions and rulings are more easily pinned to a noticeboard than told to individuals concerned in person. Admittedly, the administrative librarian or supervisor in a large library has less time to communicate orally to all staff than his counterpart in a small system, yet such written methods are likely to be ineffective.

The number of staff employed and their physical distribution may dictate, say, use of the telephone as a substitute for face-to-face communication. Thus, for example, in Birmingham Public Library, with a staff of 482 (March 1972) leavers are more frequently spoken to by the librarian or deputy by telephone than interviewed face-to-face. Similarly, certain situations may dictate a choice of spoken communication; in instances of counselling, of helping staff with emotional difficulties which are affecting their work, purposes can scarcely be achieved by utilisation of written communication. This is particularly so where non-directive counselling is employed, that is where an emphasis is placed on open discussion, on relieving frustration and personal adjustment, rather than a statement of diagnosis of the problem and the offering of advice which is the pattern of directive counselling.

So far as the general trend of communication is concerned, that is where means is not rigidly conditioned in the above manner by variables of purpose, oral communication should be favoured in libraries except where routine administrative matters or supportive written records are concerned. The reason for this statement is that oral communication enables the senior staff to become familiar with individual members of staff, their attitudes and enthusiasms, and to promote such enthusiasm by treating members of staff as individuals and according their ideas serious attention.

Gesture

In speech, individuals use two kinds of signs to reinforce what they are saying. These signs are auditory and gestural. Auditory signs relate to tone and include rasping and emotion. Gestural signs emanate from many parts of the body, most normally from the face or hands. It is still possible to employ auditory signs in speech delivered over the telephone but obviously not possible to use gestural signs. English speaking peoples regard any great display of activity to reinforce the spoken word as unusual and often embarrassing, yet such signs do help to extend the communicative character of speech to indicate precise or subtle shades of meaning.

Of course, just as it is possible to communicate meaning and feelings by silence, so it is possible to communicate by the use of signs alone, such as a nod or pointed finger. Yet face-to-face communication of any length must usually employ a combination of gesture and speech or speech alone. The words we use can be effectively supported or contradicted by what we say with our own physical movements, just as what we understand by what we hear can be extended by what we observe in the speaker (Lamb 33). Gestures are used to illustrate, to emphasise, to point, to explain or to interpret and therefore cannot be isolated from the verbal components of speech.

Telephone

Many misunderstandings or annoyances resulting from telephone conversations relate to conversations between strangers. Thus, taking the example of external library communication, a person might be annoyed by what he considers to be the off-handed treatment accorded to his enquiry by a member of the reference staff. Many such misunderstandings are avoided in internal communication because communicators and receivers know each other, picture each other whilst talking and each can often imagine the other person's reaction to what is said. In other words, communication is reinforced by compensatory imagined gestures and appearances. Also, telephone conversations between persons familiar with each other are less likely to be accorded an artificial element through the individual's attempts to impress by adopting a style of speech which is not normal for that person.

Telephone communication has certain advantages over face-to-face communication so far as internal staff communication is concerned. Use of the telephone usually stimulates the communicator to think about what he is going to say, to think about its purpose and content, more than in many face-to-face encounters. Secondly, it seems to encourage brevity of conversation in formal communication. There is less tendency than in face-to-face encounters to go from one subject to another and less tendency to prolong a conversation before one person actually departs physically. Disadvantages of the telephone relate to lack of written record (*ie* comparing this means with written communication) and lack of gestural reinforcement even between friends.

The main types of telephone systems used in libraries are PABX, PBX, and PAX. PABX (Private Automatic Branch Exchange) combines internal and external links on one telephone connection with another station within the library (be it in hq or a branch) and is performed through an automatic switching unit. This system, as used for example in the library of University College, Cardiff, frees the operator to give all her attention to outside calls and often enables internal links to be established faster than with certain alternative telephone systems. PBX (Private Branch Exchange), as used in Leeds University Library, combines the internal and external links but internal calls go through the manual switchboard. PAX (Private Automatic Exchange) is a purely internal system similar in design to the ordinary GPO telephone network, using a central automatic exchange. This system, as in use in Luton Public Library, involves the use by staff of two telephones (*ie* two dial-type handsets, one linked to the PAX system, the other to the normal GPO receiver for outside calls).

The choice of a system may not be left entirely to the initiative or discretion of the librarian; it may be dictated by a local government or university decision on a uniform system for all local government or university departments. Whatever the basic reason for choice, however, the three systems can be modified by the use of push button handsets and loudspeakers. Normally such facilities are designed to give quick contact between a select number of staff or to ease the communication procedures for top administrative staff. At Luton Public Library, for example, the librarian and deputy have loudspeakers (with handsets as well for use on occasions when it is preferable to have at least one end of the conversation inaudible to anyone else who may be within earshot of the loudspeaker) and push button handsets. All other handsets are equipped with three press buttons, one providing direct access to the librarian, one to the deputy and the third being used with a dialled number to provide contact with all other stations.

Use of the telephone in libraries as an alternative to face-to-face communication is marked where geographic distance makes face-to-face communication impossible or unrealistic. Between departments or persons located in the same building it facilitates speed of communication, cuts down on physical movement and can be used in conjunction with face-to-face communication, to summon or request a person's appearance in a particular department or before a particular person. Used in this manner there seems no danger or tendency in replacing face-to-face communication with telephone conversation in situations that should require face-to-face discussion; there is not the same inclination, as may be evident in external communication, to take advantage of lack of personal contact and shelter behind the cloak of partial anonymity which the telephone affords.

b) Spoken communication to groups

Group meetings have a number of purposes, some of which can be identified as advantages to be gained from the use of oral group communication. These purposes include the quick interchange of facts and opinions, this process often being conducive to change and progress; the stimulation and shaping of ideas; the commitment of a number of people to given proposals; and the utilisation of wide sources of knowledge and experience possessed by members of the group that it is not normally possible for one person to acquire. Addition may also be made of more specific purposes or advantages. One of the purposes of staff meetings in Lancashire County Library is staff training; it is felt that the more junior staff have much to gain from such meetings not only in factual information but also in witnessing processes relating to library decision making and participating in discussion.

The main disadvantages of group meetings are that they are time-consuming, cause delay in action and override individual opinions or level them to compromise solutions and recommendations, such compromise reflecting mediocrity rather than excellence. Meetings are more time consuming than individual conferences in so far as they involve a higher figure of man hours. Whether such time is wasteful in relation to achieved results is often a matter of opinion and an area in which the chairman must seek to provide realistic guidance in, for example, cutting short prolonged discussions on a particular matter or cutting short a verbose individual.

It is often argued that group or committee meetings cause delay because members will shelve an action or decision till the next meeting. This disadvantage, such an approach to action and decisions, is partly a reflection of individual dispositions. Some people will find it convenient to adopt such delaying tactics as an excuse for not taking immediate action. The disadvantage may partly be resolved by defining as clearly as possible the areas of subject interest of the particular regular meeting and its areas of authority; such definitions may help to provide an indication of the type of matter which should be the subject of day-to-day decision making and action.

The mediocrity of compromise and solutions is a serious criticism of group meetings. Here again, however, the chairman bears a responsibility to seek out what he considers to be the best solution, not necessarily that reflecting the greatest consensus. Secondly, it may be said that the chairman or person responsible for taking a particular decision or action does not necessarily have to accept the committee recommendations or suggestions; he should balance compromise against quality decision and action.

In considering the purposes or aims of group meetings, attention should also be focused on factors which are more immediately linked to the overall purpose of achieving levels of library service and goals. Such purposes are three in number:

1 To inform. The librarian, or chairman of the meeting, may simply present information in the form of 'state of the library report' or summary of library committee deliberations. In such a report he may inform staff of developments resulting from decisions already taken. Alternatively, although the librarian or chairman may already have made certain decisions or taken certain actions, as well as informing he may invite reactions, hoping that this will prompt approval of his decisions or actions.

2 To discuss. The librarian or chairman may put certain facts to his staff. These facts may relate to a particular problem; he may pose a number of possible solutions to this problem as he sees it and invite discussion on these. Individual members may be encouraged to present papers on a particular subject or give an account of recent activities in their departments and ideas for future development, such presentation to be followed by general discussion. Lancaster University Library encourages the presentation of papers at its senior staff meetings (*eg* Sept 1971, to consider a 'rolling' short loan period), the papers often being circulated before the meeting; while senior staff meetings at Luton Public Library often include presentations by heads of departments. These presentations to some extent fall into the general pattern of staff meeting subject content—largely topics arising from working situations—but do provide the opportunity for wider discussion of library policy.

3 To consult. The librarian or chairman may pose a problem and invite ideas on possible solutions.

The degree of emphasis given in any library to one or more of these purposes is very much conditioned by the management style of the chief librarian and the value he attaches to such meetings and staff participation.

The anticipated result of the meeting, that is to say the result as anticipated by its convener, forms part of the purpose in any of the three categories given above. Such results are often described as problem solving or decision taking. It should be borne in mind, though, that however united the consensus of opinion among a group of people and however closely this opinion is followed, decisions and administrative actions are taken by one person rather than by a group. Hence, rather than saying that the group or com-

90

mittee solve a problem or take a decision, it is more accurate to say that suggestions are made as to the best or advisable courses of action and that the librarian, chairman or responsible person initiates action to solve a problem or makes a decision on the basis of such suggestions. This process is particularly noticeable where the group is an advisory committee or working group and where it reports to the librarian or other senior person. Thus the advisory functions and group deliberations of the Library of Congress Human Relations Committees and Council contrasts with the executive decision taking of the librarian or heads of departments to whom matters may be referred (Library of Congress).

The purposes of a meeting are linked to the size of the participating or attending group, which in turn is often related to the type of membership, *eg* whole library, departmental or cross sectional, such as working groups. A Irving's studies of industrial communication leads him to conclude that if a group comprises less than five members it may never witness a critical approach to problems, since one member will not spark off another. Above twenty the group becomes a mass meeting and the optimum number for a meeting where questions have to be asked and answered and discussion entered into is between twenty five and thirty (Irving 120). The research of R F Bales indicates that if membership rises above seven, communication becomes centralised because members do not have adequate opportunity to communicate directly with each other (Bales). One danger of larger groups is that speakers tend to address their communication to persons deemed to be the most powerful or interested in the activity of the group and that sub-group factions and allegiances might develop. Another danger is that the larger the group the less chance will there be of fully utilising the resources of individual members.

In libraries the optimum number of members of a working group seems to lie between twelve and fifteen. Disadvantages relating to size are one reason, other than those relating to level of staff activity and responsibility, why in medium and large-sized libraries separate staff meetings tend to be held for senior and junior staff. An alternative, less common, form of arrangement is to hold meetings of staff and departmental representatives, as opposed to all staff or all staff in a particular category or department. Sheffield University Library Staff Committee, for example, which meets three times a year, consists of representatives of all grades of staff including attendants and has a membership of fourteen representing a staff of eighty (March 1972).

So far as ad hoc departmental meetings and working groups are concerned, the frequency with which meetings are held depends on circumstances of need and staff availability. In the case of routine or regular meetings (*eg* monthly staff meetings for senior staff), it is advisable that they should follow a known and established pattern regarding date and time. Accepting the fact that this may result in some delayed action, an advantageous result will be that staff will prepare for these meetings, often by simply making a mental note to raise a matter which does not require more urgent attention. To hold general staff meetings irregularly, perhaps at short notice or even without the guarantee of a further meeting at all, is to negate much of their value and is one indication that the librarian or convener favours the inform or tell style of management. Alternatively, it is an indication that in a small library communication is quite informal and that more formal staff meetings are considered necessary only as circumstances or demand requires.

The arrangements for staff meetings in any particular library can be comprehensive and quite complex, especially in a large system, as may be seen from the following example relating to Leeds City Libraries:

1 Heads of central departments meetings

Heads of departments have scheduled monthly meetings with the city librarian and deputy. A formal agenda is prepared and minutes taken. Subjects discussed concern both departmental and inter-departmental policy and objectives.

2 Branch librarians meetings

Scheduled monthly meeting with the city librarian and deputy.

3 Book selection meeting

Scheduled weekly meeting with heads of central departments and branch librarians.

4 Working parties

eg Cataloguing Working Party. An ad hoc group under the chairmanship of the city librarian. Currently considering the future cataloguing policy and revision implementation problems.

5 Larger central departments have monthly staff meetings. No formal agenda is prepared or minutes taken. Topics discussed include feedback from heads of central departments meetings and day-to-day working problems.

Libraries of all sizes should hold regular group or staff meetings, their composition (*eg* general; departmental; functional, *ie* subject) and frequency depending on the size of the library and hence its organisational structure and upon the present state of communication within the library. A new chief librarian in a particular library might, for example, hold a number of quickly successive meetings in an attempt to establish good communications.

In libraries examined for this study a rather neglected category of meetings is the monthly meeting between the librarian and deputy with departmental/service/regional heads. Otherwise, the major group of staff who should occasion more attention in libraries, from the point of view of group meetings, is junior staff (professional and non-professional). Some libraries hold combined senior and junior staff meetings (*eg* Leeds University Library, 3 pa). Birmingham Public Library is restructuring its irregular junior meetings according to a more regular pattern, establishing meetings run by junior staff themselves. This is an interesting development but needs to be linked to adequate feedback of discussion to senior staff or supplementary joint staff meetings; otherwise junior staff may just tend to air views and complaints to their own captive audience in a vacuum. Joint meetings are to be preferred for another reason. Junior staff are always intensely curious as to the proceedings of senior staff meetings and hence there is an interest and atmosphere conducive to effective communication down to the junior staff. In the Library of UMIST juniors became dissatisfied with their own separate meetings and their preferred type of combined meetings are now held every four to six months.

Not all matters which may be discussed at senior staff meetings can be discussed at combined meetings. Such matters may relate to junior efficiency or rotation. In view of this fact and in view of the size of numbers involved in large libraries, many libraries have decided against combined meetings. Such decisions are reasonable but attention should still be given to junior staff communication in the form of publicity and distribution of committee discussions from which they are excluded and which are not of a confidential or restricted nature.

These stipulations relating to publicity and distribution of deliberations are important in so far as any group meeting, other than whole library meetings, is concerned. It is important not only for the librarian or senior staff to utilise committee deliberations in their decision making but also to extend the communicative act stimulated by group discussion to all staff whose duties or interests cover relevant topics.

Some libraries encourage staff (usually senior staff) who have attended meetings to communicate relevant discussion and points of information to their colleagues or staff in their own department. Admittedly, this process can be hampered by lack of time or individual lack of enthusiasm. The Applied Physics Laboratory Library of the Johns Hopkins University initiated weekly meetings attended by professional staff. ' It was hoped that the information exchanged would in turn be relayed by the attendees to other workers in their respective projects' (Schulz & Kepple 151). It became apparent, however, that this did not always succeed. Hence transcripts were made of the meetings and from them abridged versions were prepared for distribution to all members of staff; such abridgements formed the genesis of the *APL library staff newsletter*. If at all practicable, however, emphasis should be placed on oral reporting to departmental groups and where necessary to individual members of staff. Such processes will facilitate the extension of communication on a library-wide basis and link the individual and group methods of oral communication.

Written communication

As with spoken communication, it is not proposed in this chapter to give detailed guidance or information on techniques of communication or actual presentation of material. Many guides exist to clear and successful writing (Gunning), analysing the composition of language and sentence structure in the light of criteria of clarity and ease of reading. Suffice it to say here that the communicator should always consider his purpose in communicating, the people he is aiming his communication at and its possible effects on others who may read it, and he should attempt to communicate in a manner which will be understood. The tone of the communication may be as informal or as formal as the situation dictates.

Written communication possesses one clear advantage over spoken communication: in spoken communication it is not always possible to give time and thought to preparation, to the organisation of what one is going to say and its content. With written communication, however hastily contrived, second thoughts or a few moments of planning are usually possible. Providing one is using

94

appropriate language the results should usually achieve a greater degree of clarity and meaning than spoken communication. That this is not always so is due to a number of factors. These include the lack of immediate feedback, instant amendment of communication and reinforcement of communication through gesture— factors which do exist in a situation of spoken communication. Furthermore, effectiveness of written communication may suffer since the receiver may be adversely affected by the personal or work status characteristics of the communicator, although the incidence of this should not be as great as with spoken communication. Similarly, the receiver may react negatively towards the means of communication before actually reading it; a person subject to a constant stream of memos and letters may well fail to give due attention to the contents of each item he receives.

Other advantages which written communication possesses over spoken communication relate to usage of this means. It is better, that is its effect is likely to be greater and its purpose achieved, in certain circumstances and for certain tasks. Thus written communication is better for presenting detailed and complex information. It is used with value to confirm or verify details communicated orally, especially where the information may be constantly referred to. It can present stored information, the content of which does not change in time in the sense that memories of spoken communication fade or a spoken instruction or piece of information possibly change if relayed from one person to another.

The main circumstances in which written communication may be used with advantage can be tabulated as follows:

1 Where permanence is required. Instructions written into memos or staff manuals, although requiring occasional alteration in face of changing conditions, combat personal and staff characteristics such as fading memories and staff changes.

2 Where uniformity is required. Written instructions and information, if authoritatively written and if their source (eg chief librarian) is clearly indicated, help to eliminate many arguments or quandaries relating to differences of opinion and genuine uncertainty. Such arguments and uncertainties could admittedly be eliminated by spoken communication delivered at, say, a staff meeting. If, however, it is difficult to assemble all staff concerned or it is thought that the disadvantage of this so far as staff time and travelling expenses are concerned would be greater than any

advantages involved, written communication is appropriate in these circumstances, especially if the factor of permanence is also involved. Thus Harvard University Library, comprising some 90 separate libraries or departments, possesses no single classification scheme and no unified code common to all its libraries. In 1960 it published a guide for departmental libraries concerning the relationship of their cataloguing to the central library. This guide was prepared at the specific request of a number of departmental library cataloguers and contains information on the preparation of entries for the union catalogue, consultation of the union catalogue, and so on.

Somewhat paradoxically, written communication may also be favoured where it is necessary to clarify or arrange variations, as opposed to uniformity, in procedures. Thus in Flintshire County Library written communication is used for instructions and information relating to duties necessitating variations, *eg* transfers, temporary assignments, sick leave pay and so on. Where variation is constant or frequent, standard circulars may be misleading. In Liverpool University Library, for example, where the education library has different opening hours from the main library, it is sometimes necessary to draft special instructions for the departmental library. Such variations in procedure are usually of a comparatively routine nature and may conveniently be linked with point 6 below.

3 Where geographic dispersal of staff makes spoken communication, save perhaps by telephone, difficult. One means of written communication used in many county libraries in Britain (*eg* Flintshire) or large municipal systems (*eg* Camden), for comparatively routine matters such as reservation or reference requests, is telex.

4 Where detailed information is to be passed from one person to another, and where the receiver is to work on or with the information. Into this category would fall annual departmental reports submitted to the librarian to facilitate the compilation of the library's annual report.

5 Where it is necessary to pass information to a number of people and to get their considered comments on it. Thus proposals for a new staff structure could be passed to a number of persons, each person adding his written comments.

6 Where the content is comparatively routine (*eg* holiday closing

arrangements) and where it may be necessary for receivers to return a signed chit to the sender.

7 As an alternative to spoken communication: a) Where it is felt that written communication can save time compared with spoken communication, without loss of effect. The most obvious instance of this in libraries relates to staff news sheets. Small libraries, with an informal atmosphere and constant oral inter-communication, usually find it unnecessary to have news sheets. Larger libraries find them a useful supplement to staff meetings, for the presentation of some of the more routine, though not necessarily uninteresting, library news. b) Where it is desired to keep a matter impersonal, to avoid personality clashes and time-consuming argument. Thus if a matter such as staff restructuring has occasioned heated argument at library staff meetings, the librarian might find it advisable to circulate factual information in a written form for individual consideration.

Apart from the librarian's view of communication and his general style of management, the most important factors determining the volume of written as opposed to spoken communication in the libraries studied are:

a) size and geographic dispersal of the library (*eg* Liverpool University library)

b) whether the communication is to a single individual or a number of persons; if the former, spoken communication is favoured (*eg* Durham University Library)

c) content of communication—written communication is favoured for routine matters in all save the smallest libraries which operate on a basic oral staff inter-communication system.

Most of the categories 1 to 7 above involve communication to numbers of staff as opposed to single individuals and it does seem to be the pattern in libraries that most communication to individual members of staff is spoken. This is desirable anyway from the point of view of staff relations. Written communications to individuals, that is to just one other person in the library, either confirm orders and information conveyed orally or are of a basically routine nature. In the larger library written communication to individuals takes on a greater importance or volume, even though it may be confined to comparatively routine matters, such as instructions to reply to a request for information received from a reader or interested person. Such written communication may take the form of papers which are received by the library from an outside source and simply passed on by, say, the librarian to a member of staff whose duties and/or interests are relevant to the subject content of the material. Luton Public Library has usefully prepared circulation slips to facilitate such a distribution of material.

The volume of horizontal written communication is limited in most libraries of whatever type and size compared with horizontal spoken communication. This is true also of upward communication, written communication being largely confined to regular routine reports from departmental heads or senior staff to the librarian or deputy.

Written communication, down to the individual as a single person or one of a group of persons, begins when he or she reads a job advertisement in a newspaper or periodical and supplements this by a detailed examination of job particulars sent from the library at his request. Such particulars should include as full an account of the job as possible, including details of salary range, precise working hours and so on. Presentation of such detail will enable the reader to build up as accurate as possible a picture of the job and save him asking for information on these details at the interview, which should supplement the written particulars by providing the interviewee with an awareness of promotion prospects, levels of responsibility and library policies.

The written announcements or job descriptions read by a potential member of staff provide one example of written communication which is directed from the library to an outside community and is not therefore strictly speaking part of staff communication. Nevertheless, it often comes to the attention of present members of staff. Other examples relate to library news contained in local newspapers and in library committee minutes. Local newspapers are obviously purchased by many members of the staff or their families and are available in public library reading rooms. Public library committee minutes (*ie* normally the report of the committee which is moved and adopted at council meetings) are usually available in reference libraries where they can be read by members of staff as well as members of the public and many library committees are open to the public and press. University library committee minutes are often available for consultation by staff from their library representative (*eg* Keele University) or the library secretary (*eg* Leeds University), or may be circulated among senior library staff (*eg* Durham

University). Yet in the case of both press reports and library committee minutes it can be a shock to a member of staff to read something about the library in such sources, especially if it affects his department or duties and he has had no warning of their contents. Chief librarians obviously cannot always be aware of what is going to appear in the press and may not be able to discuss library committee matters with staff until the committee has actually sat. In Sheffield, for example, the press is given a statement after meetings of the Sheffield City Libraries and Arts Committee. Thus a news item sometimes appears the next morning before the library staff can be informed. Yet if the librarian cannot prevent staff shocks at least he should attempt to prevent staff anger or dissatisfaction which may result from such shock. He can do this by an adequate general communication programme and by discussing matters which appear in the press or library committee minutes with relevant staff immediately after the appearance of the item in print.

If the material content is non-controversial, the librarian should still cater for his staff's information needs and curiosity by regularly reporting on library committee matters or a selection of the most important in summary form. This may be done at staff meetings (*eg* at Newcastle University Library, staff meetings, about five per annum, are geared to the programme of library committee meetings. These staff meetings are attended by senior staff plus representatives of juniors, bindery and clerical staff) or as an item in the library staff news sheet (*eg* North Riding County Library and Edinburgh University Library). Similarly, non-controversial press reports may be noted or summarised in a library staff news sheet (*eg* Surrey County Library staff news sheet includes notes or summaries of library items appearing in the local press and periodicals such as *Surrey life*).

Forms of written communication
One form of written communication, regularly produced in most libraries, is the annual report. This is nominally a report to the library committee and hence may also be viewed as communication aimed at the community outside the immediate confines of the library staff. In public libraries the report, as is the case very often with library committee proceedings, is usually summarised in the local press. In this case again it is useful to staff and a sign of consideration by the librarian, if copies are distributed to all

99

members of staff. If cost makes this uneconomic copies should at least be circulated to heads of departments and other senior staff and these persons encouraged to report on the matter to their staff. Such arrangements are operated at Surrey County Library. Alternative arrangements might be for a special summary of the full report to be produced for distribution to all staff as a separate publication or as a major item on a staff news sheet. Other alternative arrangements are to make the report available to all staff on request (*eg* Bucks County Library), possibly displaying specimen copies in the staff room for inspection (*eg* Warwick University Library) or to have copies circulated (*eg* Bradford University Library).

The most important forms of written communication which are directed primarily at library staff comprise memoranda and reports, staff handbooks and manuals, news sheets and magazines, and noticeboards. The remaining part of this chapter is primarily taken up with an examination of these various forms.

Memoranda and reports
In commercial and industrial organisations, memoranda and reports are often the main form of written communication. In libraries the general position is by no means so certain. Much information may be conveyed in a staff news sheet and, in fact, the situation varies a great deal amongst libraries. Sometimes memoranda are labelled 'administrative memos', conveying instructions and being designed to supplement and bring up-to-date existing staff manuals (*eg* Bootle Public Library's Staff Instructions form a procedure manual); in such circumstances, being linked to a staff manual, memos may lose much of their precise definition as a separate form of written communication.

Both memoranda and reports convey information, report findings, put forward ideas and may make recommendations. Both form the basis for future decision making and action. This may be immediately apparent: a librarian may order a change in the circulation system as a result of a report from the lending librarian. Alternatively, the effect on decision making or action may be disguised and less obvious: a monthly report from a branch librarian, containing mainly a presentation of statistical data, may not trigger off immediate decisions by the librarian but could form the basis of long-term thought and ultimately decisions concerning that branch or a number of service points.

100

The structure of a memorandum and report may be similar, presenting a definition of the subject and statement of objectives, a presentation of facts relating to a situation, plus an indication of possible solutions or courses of action and recommendations. Furthermore, as with all forms of written communication, the compiler of the memorandum or report should aim for accuracy, brevity and clarity, paying due attention to the processes of preparation, arrangement, writing and revision.

Memoranda and reports do differ, however, not only perhaps in their size but as concerns the circumstances which provoke them. Memoranda are often shorter than reports, being roughly the equivalent of internal letters, but usually being directed at all staff or groups rather than individuals. They are often linked to oral means of communication, providing a record of discussions or decisions made as a result of the discussions. Furthermore, unless they are routine memoranda (*eg* containing instructions on fire drill), they are normally written under pressure of time, in response to particular circumstances. In contrast, many reports are of a routine nature; although they may be linked to the time factor (*eg* monthly reports) their compilation is often seen as being less urgent than the compilation of a memorandum.

The original meaning of a memorandum was ' a note to help the memory '; to this function has been added those of conveying information and instructions, that is new information and instructions, and making proposals for future action. Thus, although S Eilon defines a memorandum as ' a message that provides information, not as part of a routine procedure ' (Eilon 120), if ' information ' is interpreted in part as ' instruction ', then the routine element is bound to be evident. Birmingham University Library has produced a ten page duplicated document entitled *Routine for counter staff on evening duty,* setting out duties (*eg* checking vouchers) and procedures for particular occurrences (*eg* in relation to handicapped persons). If this is to be regarded as a memorandum then instruction must be included in one's definition.

Reports involve a larger element of upward communication than do memoranda and their timing is usually predictable in the sense that they are required by such a date or after a certain period or completion of a particular task. The content of routine reports is usually information, although recommendations and opinions may be contained in a non-routine report. For example, a report to the librarian on a course of library instruction held for external groups such as school children or local industrialists could include suggestions from the organiser as to the content and arrangement of future courses of a similar nature.

Eilon usefully distinguishes between time-triggered reports and event-triggered reports (Eilon 120). Routine reports such as monthly branch library reports fall within the first category; reports following the completion of tasks or events come into the second category. Their detail depends on circumstances and subject, and the formality of their presentation may depend upon the approach to report writing of the individual person and their purpose. If the librarian requires a report, which he in turn desires to present to his library committee, he may require more detail and greater formality of presentation than might normally be the case. The general value of reports, as opposed to memoranda and other forms of written communication, is that they increase people's awareness of what is required of them in their work or what is happening in the library. As a result they increase the rationality of people's decisions and the efficiency of their actions.

Staff handbooks and manuals

Staff handbooks, of value not only to the new member of staff but also as a source of reference for the established member, do not aim at presenting procedural details relating to individual jobs or departments of the library—that is more properly the function of a staff manual. What a handbook should attempt to do is to provide brief details of what the library is and its purpose in a wider community or academic or industrial environment, of staff relationships (*eg* with supervisors and readers) and responsibilities, work schedules (number of hours worked per week, etc) and holidays, salaries, staff facilities (*eg* common rooms, educational courses) and professional organisations and trade unions.

Some new members of library staff are presented with a handbook relating to the wider organisation of which the library is a part. Examples are to be found in all types of libraries, relating to the industrial company, the university or the local government authority. All new junior staff at Birmingham Public Library, for example, are given a copy of *Forward: a handbook for junior entrants,* which outlines the functions of Birmingham Corporation, indicates what is expected of new staff during a six months' probationary period and gives details of conditions of work, holidays, salary, trade union membership and a code of professional conduct. Such a handbook is useful and saves the library itself a lot of time in presenting such information. Nevertheless, this general type of organisational handbook should be supplemented by information more relevant to library staff. In the case of Birmingham Public Libraries the Corporation handbook is supplemented by a library *Staff handbook*, giving information on Birmingham Public Libraries, conditions of service, fire precautions, links with other libraries, Nalgo and Birmingham Public Library Staff Association and Benevolent Society, as well as an organisation chart and a list of library officers, plus departmental addresses and telephone numbers.

The handbook should be written so as to emphasise the duties and privileges of individual members of staff, attempting to stress the relative importance of the individual. It should be written in as informal and friendly a manner as is consistent with dignity and authority, and statutory requirements, relating to the provision of employee information on such matters as hours of work, detailed in the 1963 *Contracts of employment act*. The introduction should pay particular attention to the new member of staff. This is admirably done, for example, in the New York Public Library staff handbook.

As with any form of written communication, the handbook should be as well produced as time and money allow, since it will help condition the impressions gained by the new member of staff and should form a permanent source of reference during his or her period of employment at the library. Such functions will be best achieved if the handbook is produced with the format of a handbook and not, say, A4 duplicated sheets, and a cover that can stand up to a certain amount of wear. Such a handbook has been produced by Brooklyn Public Library. A convenient size ($5\frac{1}{4}$in by $8\frac{1}{4}$in, 16 pages) it is attractively produced on good quality paper with a designed cover and contains information clearly presented in green type on yellow paper.

As indicated in an earlier section of this chapter, many memoranda, especially those designated ' administrative memoranda ', provide information and instruction on library procedures. If, however, they are numerous they may lead to confusion through sheer volume, even though they may be well produced and numbered to facilitate filing. Most libraries will find it convenient and advantageous to present the information on procedures (plus possibly certain areas of policy as well) in a more systematic form of a staff manual. This is best produced in a loose-leaf form to allow for revision and additions, possibly by means of memoranda, with tables of contents and index, if possible, to facilitate use.

The general advantages of having a staff manual in any library are as follows:

1 Duties, responsibilities and relationships are assigned, helping to avoid overlap, duplication of effort, friction and staff uncertainty.

2 Procedures are detailed. This helps establish uniformity throughout the system and provides a permanent source of reference, which is particularly helpful during periods of staff turnover and relief. In addition, such detailing of procedures provides an authoritative supplement to instruction and information given by oral means. The elimination of indecision will not necessarily involve the elimination of initiative. A staff manual, while perhaps presenting information on library policy, is basically concerned with procedural details; there is normally no suggestion that professional initiative is unnecessary or restricted by the existence of a staff manual. This situation could be made clear by distinguishing between mandatory and discretionary instructions or indicating that department heads have some discretion in interpreting rules, subject to the proviso that all departures from normal practice be discussed with the librarian. The latter proviso, for example, is stated in the introduction to Reading University Library's *Notes for staff.*

3 It may encourage the individual member of staff to take a broader view of the library and its activities than his own immediate duties and department dictate, and promote understanding among staff scattered over a wide geographic area. This may result from a presentation of duties and responsibilities of other departments plus general library policy.

4 The compilation and revision of the manual should involve a critical reappraisal of duties and procedures, facilitating the removal of irregularities and outmoded elements and giving the compilers a greater understanding of their work.

The chief librarian is probably too far removed from day-to-day operations to be able to write all sections of a general staff manual. Hence it is advisable that people performing particular tasks should write the first drafts of sections or chapters of the manual. In a large system these could be collated by department or service heads, before being passed to the librarian or senior administrative editor of the final manual. In smaller systems, department heads could compile the first drafts, passing them direct to the librarian, perhaps after discussion with their staffs.

The manual can be as brief or as inclusive as desired; it can relate to the whole library or individual departments or services. The medium or large library will probably find it advisable to maintain a general manual outlining library policy and procedures for, say, such matters as staff appointment and leave, plus a number of department or service manuals. The maintenance of a complete and very detailed manual covering all the library service and procedures, copies being deposited in all departments and at all service points, is a somewhat extravagant provision and basically unnecessary. As a general rule a clear definition of content and audience will safeguard a manual from excessive detail, covering, say, all possible variations of an activity and rare circumstances, which is one of the chief causes of premature obsolescence and complicated appearance of manuals.

The maintenance of a detailed manual is mainly justified in a system where general service units or points, that is units or departments not arranged on the basis of subject or service alone, are scattered over a wide geographic area, many staff at a particular point or within a particular region never visiting other points or headquarters and not being transferred to such points. In these circumstances a detailed manual is not only a guide to procedures but provides staff with a picture of what happens in other localities.

These conditions obviously apply in the British county system. Staffordshire County Library maintains a very detailed manual, comprising 200 pages of duplicated material in loose-leaf form. In contrast, Gloucestershire County Library has produced a comparatively short manual of 32 pages. Save for the section on adult mobile libraries procedure, which details duties (*eg* ' The librarian assists the driver when reversing and on all difficult roads. He/she will get out of the mobile onto the road in order to advise the driver '), the manual lays down general policy and outlines procedures.

Such a manual is especially useful for introducing the new member of staff to the system and in creating an awareness of procedures and responsibilities in other sections of the library. It would, however, obviously need supplementing by more detailed departmental or service manuals, instruction sheets or continual oral instruction.

All manuals, whether library-wide or departmental, should comprise sections compiled basically from the functional point of view (*eg* accessions, cataloguing, circulation) of duties and service, rather than from the point of view of the duties of an individual. The latter may be indicated in functional divisions and such divisions will obviously be related to individual departments (*eg* cataloguing, reference library). To these sections could be added a short one on staff obligations and responsibilities toward library users and service. Such a section helps link expressions of an individual library policy and staff responsibilities to the more general concept of the library profession and is usefully included in, for example, Lanark County Library staff manual. A more lengthy statement of standards of service and on relations with the public is to be found in the staff manual of the Enoch Pratt Free Library. In this library's manual the section on Pratt Library Standards covers three pages and has the advantage, so far as staff acceptance is concerned, of being prepared by a staff committee.

Another general addition is a statement of the function of the manual or an indication of its importance and relation to other means of communication, such as oral instruction by supervisory staff or other types of staff manual. Such statements are provided in the staff manuals of Staffordshire and Wiltshire County Libraries. Other additional sections may relate to more specific details, such as a directory of library departments, service points, names of departmental heads and telephone numbers. Such a list forms an appendix to Glamorgan County's *Staff manual for part time branch librarians* (1968).

All sections should be numbered in a way that will allow for insertion of revised and fresh material. Continuous numbering would be disrupted by insertions, so it is preferable to number each section with a different form of notation for the pages of each section (*eg* A. 1, 2, 3, etc; or 1. i, ii, iii, etc).

Most staff manuals present information and instruction in narrative, albeit, tabulated form. An alternative approach, which is being experimented with by Leicestershire County Library, is to present details of procedures in the form of flow charts or in diagrammatic form. Such presentation has much to commend it from the point of view of clarity, where detailed instructions are concerned, and if supplemented by general narrative on staff manual function, library objectives and staff responsibilities, could form a more attractive manual and facilitate staff understanding and ease of reference. Since understanding should be related to current procedures it is, of course, necessary to keep any form of manual under constant review. This in turn will help staff maintain a critical view of duties, responsibilities and procedures, which a manual attempts to define and detail, and will help prevent an undue increase in the degree of centralisation of decision making which may be one result of the publication of a staff manual.

News sheets and magazines
The functions and purposes of a staff news sheet or magazine are basically:

1 to communicate routine announcements (*eg* holiday dates; new appointments)

2 to feature background explanations of policy or service matters (*eg* definitions of university library authorised users, which may be written down elsewhere, such as in a staff manual or memo, but which are important enough to require occasional highlighting to serve as a reminder to staff and an introduction to new staff)

3 to promote better relations between the library administrators and remaining staff by providing explanations of policy and general library information

4 to create interest and enthusiasm in library activities by spotlighting personal achievements (*eg* examination successes) and departmental achievements (*eg* publications). Such activities and achievements may be those which take place in the outside world (*eg* the librarian's appointment to membership of a Library Association Committee) or be of national or international significance.

5 to encourage participation, if only in thinking about library matters, by all staff; in a practical manner by actively seeking contributions from all levels of staff. This is essential however formal the news sheet; one whose contents comprise only directives from the top will tend to be ignored by many staff and is hardly conducive to the encouragement of participation. The latter can be encouraged if a certain amount of opinion, even controversy, is included;

this may be regarded as feedback, valuable comment by staff on library policy and arrangements. The librarian may, through the medium of the staff news sheet, directly ask for staff opinions or assistance on a particular matter. Thus a 1971 issue of Leeds University Library's staff news sheet, *Library news,* contained the librarian's request for suggestions from staff on how to overcome the difficulty found by readers in distinguishing staff from other library users. To encourage such participation it is essential that a copy of the staff news sheet or magazine be given to all members of staff

6 to provide one communication link between staff scattered by geographic distance. This function was boldly expressed in the November 1971 issue of *Compost,* magazine of Leeds City Libraries, ' for the staff, by the staff ':

'. . . the editors firmly believe that the survival of Compost for nearly four years indicates that there is a need for this type of publication which carries news to all parts of the system and allows every member of staff to put his point of view openly in print. The great pity of the present situation is that the sense of isolation which exists in parts of the system has never been reduced by any official circulars other than the rare memos and regular interloans list. When as librarians we boast that we know what is going on in the world around us, it comes as something of a shock to come across the lack of communication which exists within our own city system.' (page 1)

7 to provide news of professional activities, trade union or library.

A staff magazine, sometimes a ' staff guild magazine ', usually differs from a staff news sheet, being a more substantial size and including articles and letters from staff describing or expressing views on an aspect of library service or staff experience, such as attendance at an outside course. The library should attempt to define the function of its news sheet and magazine, this definition providing some guidance as to the selection of content and frequency. The defined function of New York Public Library's *Staff news* is to act as an official administrative paper carrying general and specific notices of library, staff and related public events. All members of staff may contribute items, particularly those regarding their own activities. Policies, plans and occasionally directives may be presented through the *Staff news* (New York Public Library 34).

The function of Luton Public Library's staff news sheet is to communicate more formal matters directly related to library work and to exclude lengthy articles and staff letters. The latter appear in a separate staff guild magazine. Since the function of the news sheet is to provide up-to-date information to staff, its frequency is weekly and this partly helps to determine its size, which is usually one sheet printed on one or both sides. Size of publication is also in part determined by number of staff and geographic distribution. A small or medium-sized library, relying on spoken communication for the transmission of orders and news, may find it necessary to issue a news sheet only four or six times a year if at all. The larger system will most likely favour a weekly presentation or monthly presentation of a magazine.

Choice of editor for the news sheet or magazine will depend on its function. If it is a formal news sheet then the editor will normally be a senior member of staff (*eg* Luton Public Library— chief assistant). If a magazine style is favoured, the editor will often be a less senior member of staff, say, an assistant librarian, possibly aided by an editorial committee (*eg* Leeds University Library *Library news* is edited by two assistant librarians). In either case the success of the publication in good measure depends on the enthusiasm and initiative of the editor in presenting interesting and worthwhile information and persuading all levels of staff to make such contributions. It will help staff awareness of the publication and copy dates if it is issued regularly, say, once a week or once a month.

The style in which the news sheet is produced will be determined by its function, its size and its frequency of issue. Other factors may be finance and typing facilities available. The most common size for library staff news sheets and staff magazines is A4. Monthly magazines often have an individually designed cover (*eg* Camden Libraries). News sheets, usually issued at more frequent intervals, normally have a duplicated or printed heading on the front sheet. If the heading is typed in the same type face as the rest of the news sheet, and the whole thing is reproduced on white paper, the effect is rather dull. Much more striking are the printed headings or mastheads used by many libraries. The *Library of Congress information bulletin,* one of the most sophisticated of its kind and familiar to many librarians the world over, uses a coloured heading. In this case the whole bulletin is printed, facilitating the use of photographs to illustrate articles and news items. A similar format is used by many American libraries (*eg* Brooklyn Public Library). A more common style in Britain is for the news sheet to be duplicated onto a prepared sheet with a printed (usually coloured) heading.

Admittedly content interest is more important than an arresting presentation. One of the most intriguing staff news sheets and one with a high level of interest content is that emanating from Reading University Library. Published monthly, it comprises on average six xeroxed pages, containing signed typed (*eg* Saturday morning duty) or handwritten (*eg* Christmas Party) notices, plus items directly reproduced from other publications or library correspondence. Such items may be cartoons. More serious examples are an extract from an OUP publication pointing out the distinction between the various imprints issued by the Press (Oxford; at the Clarendon Press; Clarendon Press Oxford, etc), and an extract from a post office guide on ' small packets ' with weight definitions and postage information. Such extracts are often annotated by the librarian or contributor. The heading on the front page of the news sheet contains the name *Library bulletin,* number and date but not the name of the library; nevertheless its make-up and contents are very clear and appealing to the reader. A further advantage is that production time must be shorter as compared with a more conventional style news sheet.

As with most other items of communication, staff news sheets and magazines should not be issued in isolation; they are closely linked to other items of communication (*eg* instructions may update staff manuals) and other means (*eg* discussion at staff meetings). The content and function of the news sheet, in particular, will in part be determined in the light of other items of communication in a library. Los Angeles Public Library, for example, issues an *Administrative bulletin,* an informational bulletin issued almost daily by the administration office to all units. Its contents include news of library and staff developments, plus information on library procedures. One result of this type of information being published in such a manner is that the *Operation LAPL,* a monthly news letter prepared by the public relations division, presents more informal news of personnel and departmental activities, plus occasional policy details.

The staff news sheet is a comparatively easy form of communication to institute and is one of the first to come to any librarian's mind if he decides he ' must do something about staff communication '. Yet it should not be regarded as a substitute for other forms of communication, particularly forms of spoken communication such as staff meetings. In the Applied Physics Laboratory Library of Johns Hopkins University the news letter is actually seen as a substitute for staff meetings. It was found that weekly meetings of professional staff did not produce adequate relay of information exchanged by the attendees to other members of staff. Hence, once it was recognised that a news letter could accomplish the purpose of communication which the meetings had been designed to fulfil, the meetings were discontinued and the news letter became a regular monthly publication (Schulz & Kepple 152).

It is difficult to compare the effects of oral and written communication, although calculations relating to time consumed are obviously much easier. If the purpose of communication is rigidly defined it may well be possible to say that one means of communication is more efficient in accomplishing this purpose than another. Normally, however, such statements are open to doubt or at least differences of opinion and the librarian should attempt to combine spoken and written means of communication, unless the content is limited and comprises, say, only routine notices.

Noticeboards

In theory, the main advantage of a noticeboard is that it enables a message to be conveyed to a large number of people without the cost and difficulties of distributing many copies of memos or holding staff meetings. Individual reactions to noticeboards vary. Usually response is a comparative lack of interest or sheer avoidance. Perhaps this is a reflection of the typical content of material posted on a board—routine administrative announcements and reminders of duties. Certainly, the pinning of notices is to be avoided, since individual inertia may entail persons not receiving information; effective communication is even more uncertain in relation to noticeboards than other forms of written communication where a paper is actually given to each person.

As a form of communication, noticeboards often suffer from disadvantages relating to:

1 poor location—in crowded busy areas or in corridors where people are not accustomed, or do not have room, to stand

2 material is hard to read due to poor placement or small type

3 outdated material is left on the board to provide undue congestion and disarray.

If attention is paid to these factors the following types of material may usefully and effectively be posted on boards:

1 Summaries and/or reminders of official notices (*eg* duty rotas), the information having previously been communicated to staff by other means. Their posting in this manner acts as a reminder and provides a source of reference.

2 Notices of meetings. These may be repeated in, say, staff news sheets. Types of meetings usually advertised on library noticeboards include professional meetings, Nalgo or other trade union meetings, staff guild meetings, library theatre events and other cultural events in the locality.

3 Letters from ex-colleagues; holiday postcards.

It often facilitates clarity and consultation of noticeboards if the board is divided up physically into, say, sections for official and unofficial notices or if noticeboards in different localities contain different types of notices. In Leeds University Library, for example, departmental noticeboards contain only official notices, while staff room boards are divided into two sections for official notices and other notices. In the Enoch Pratt Free Library, announcements and official notices are posted on bulletin boards in each department or section, while a separate board is placed near the entrance of the central library for use by staff in posting miscellaneous announcements of any kind which may be of general interest (*eg* scholarships offered by library schools, rooms to rent, typewriter for sale).

The size of a noticeboard depends on the purpose for which it is used and, of course, the amount of information the library wishes to display on it. Placement and arrangement of notices should be carefully considered and the following notes by A Irving are useful in determining such matters:

'A reader will first look at the left-hand side of a board at eye-level (about 5ft 3in/1·6m). Otherwise notices at the top of the board are read before those at the bottom. Readers will look first at the largest section of a sectional board, at a notice with ample space around it, or at a notice with some bold display or printed emphasis. Thereafter they will move to the notice next to it to the right. Notices should be designed to be read standing.

Estimates of the maximum number of words vary between twenty-five and two hundred ' (Irving 304).

One disadvantage of written, as opposed to spoken, communication (a disadvantage which was indicated earlier in this chapter) is that written communication may be ignored and hence not achieve its desired effect, because the sender is not usually present when the written communication is received and studied by one or more persons. This difficulty may be partly obviated by the logical combination of spoken and written communication, using written communication, for example, as a reinforcing device, which will modify the effect that the written communication alone would have.

Attempts should also be made to overcome the difficulty by follow-up procedures, where the sender of a communication attempts to determine that his written communication has actually been received and its contents observed and acted upon. This follow-up procedure is obviously necessary in the case of instructions or orders but it is necessary to emphasise it since many persons, not only librarians, believe that written communication is achieved simply by sending out a hand-written or typed document. The realisation that such follow-up procedures are necessary will help the communicator bear in mind and possibly review his essential purpose in communicating and his choice of means to suit this purpose.

CHAPTER SIX

When to communicate

Volume

Within a library, as the number of jobs increases to meet new requirements of service, the number of potential communication links increases with the number of staff. Between three members of staff three different communication channels can exist; between six staff there are fifteen possible channels.

Two main points may be made in relation to the above statement. Firstly, the increased number of communication channels may not be utilised (hence the above description of ' potential communication links ') and are not necessarily related to the amount of communication which should take place in a library, commensurate with certain levels of staff satisfaction and performance. Secondly, the amount of communication which takes place is not necessarily the equivalent of the amount of information being circulated. A library in which little information is circulated may, for example, witness a high level of communication, this communication comprising staff questions and requests for more information, plus opinions on communication and work situations.

The amount of communicative activity which should take place in a library depends upon the size of the establishment, the complexity of its administrative structure and the tempo of its activities during any particular period of time. A library whose administrative structure, duties or even physical building is the subject of considerable short-term change should find a need for a greater volume of communication than in more normal times, due to staff disturbance and possible unease as to what is happening.

Too much communication, often evidenced in the distribution of irrelevant information, tends to obstruct communication channels and obscure the really important matters. Equally, of course, too little communication has its dangers, including staff apathy and resentment. Lack of information or opinions can admittedly result in or from communication by passive means; agreement or indifference can both be communicated by silence but this kind of negative communication, up or down, is usually not undertaken purposefully and hence is a sign of a poor communications system.

Individuals differ remarkably in their desire for information and ideas. It is probably true to say that there are more dangers inherent in too little communication than in too much. Too little communication can lead to wrong decisions and biased manipulation of information, resulting in unwarranted personal influence. Too much may obscure the important but at least the effects can be graded. A large volume of information, for example, made available in a particular library is there if required and individuals are free to respond to it as the occasion arises, thus creating the activity of communication.

The aim so far as volume of communication is concerned should be ' to ensure an optimum flow of information—neither too little nor too much—enough to cover but not so much as to smother. The only point where adequacy of communication can be measured is in the mind of the recipient ' (Redfield 36). Hence this problem is closely linked to that of effect, discussed in an earlier chapter, and other contents of communication apart from information. Since the librarian or senior administrative staff cannot apply precise quantitative judgements in this field, they should pay as much attention to efficiency of communication as to its volume. A flood of communication can be distracting and create ambiguity rather than clarity; improved efficiency related to means of communication and direction (seeing that the right people get the information, etc, they should) may help to reduce ambiguity.

Timing

So far, discussion of when to communicate has related to volume of communication. A further important approach is the consideration of when to release a particular communication, say, information relating to future plans. The wisdom of such release is really an indication of staff skill in communication, an indication that sufficient consideration has been paid to staff needs and interests. Such skill is closely related to more general skills of management or staff administration.

A third approach to, or concept of, ' when to communicate ' is the consideration of when to communicate with members of staff during their period of employment. This consideration involves a study of regular communication, scheduled according to the needs and progress of members of staff. This is explained with a certain emphasis being applied to particular occasions or circumstances (*eg* staff training) and is explored in the remainder of this chapter.

Communication during particular occasions:
Induction
The aims of any system or period of induction relate to the individual member of staff and to the library as a whole. It is easy for those in authority and for experienced members of staff to forget how complex the library may appear to the newcomer, especially a junior with limited experiences of libraries in any capacity and perhaps with none as a worker in them. An induction course hence aims at putting the newcomer at ease and imparting a certain background knowledge relating to the library, its procedures and the employee's rights and responsibilities. The benefit to the library is that a period of induction, coupled with a more detailed period of training, leads to the employee's involvement in the library (*ie* in duties, awareness of library goals, etc), compliance with certain sets of rules and regulations and division of responsibilities, and consequent contribution to library effectiveness.

Although the term ' induction ' is sometimes defined so as to include early training, induction differs from training. Training implies the learning of skills and testing of aptitudes, induction the learning of information relating to the library and an individual job. Induction has a slightly wider conceptual meaning than ' orientation '. The latter implies adjustment to a new situation, to a new library and/or a new job, and depends as much on the attitude of the person concerned and those he meets as on the information and background details imparted. Orientation may take place over a period of one day or take the individual several months; hence it may well overlap a period of induction. The latter is designed to introduce the member of staff to a particular set of circumstances, to impart an awareness of duties and rights and so on, which are common to a number of staff.

Induction should be a relatively easy time for communication in one respect. That is that the new member of staff usually displays a high level of interest in learning about the library; he is perhaps more receptive than he will ever be and hence the communicator should have fewer problems relating to the effect of his communi-

116

cation than in many other library situations. Nevertheless, the communicator must still pay attention to the content, means and timing of his communication.

Information which the new member of staff should be given relates to:

1 the library as an organisation—how it is organised, how it operates, what it does, something of its history and goals and its personnel policies

2 the individual's job—its tasks and the member of staff's relations to colleagues, so far as responsibility and authority are concerned

3 working conditions and aids—where the member of staff's place of work is, where he gets materials necessary for the completion of his work, and working rules relating to salary, hours, coffee breaks and so on.

Some of this information will be given prior to employment, that is in job advertisements and at interviews. Much of the background information can with advantage be presented in written form, as a staff handbook (see section on staff handbooks and manuals in the previous chapter). The latter, even if supplemented by oral information and explanation, may be too detailed and slightly confusing to the new junior member of staff. For such staff some brief notes or an extended letter of welcome from the librarian might well be more appropriate and helpful. Dudley Public Library has prepared a very useful set of introductory notes for new staff. The notes comprise four duplicated sheets and present basic details under the headings of: appointment, hours, shifts, tea breaks and meals, pay, increments, calculation of earnings, holidays, compassionate leave, sickness, termination of employment, dismissal, trade union, punctuality and signing on, timesheet, grievance procedure, personal problems, tea and sugar money, staff room, staff guild, expenses, telephone calls and dress; a postscript urges new staff to consult the general office, head of department or any senior member of staff if they have any queries about job or working conditions not answered by the notes. Cheshire County Library welcomes new staff by means of a letter and attached information sheet, presenting similar types of information. The letter has the advantage of including a paragraph on the library profession and standards of service.

Such written information is best limited to background notes on the library and general conditions and procedures common to all members of staff. A major part of oral communication during induction should comprise an introduction of a new employee's specific position in the library and duties and responsibilities with his first assigned job. These are best communicated by the employee's head of department or immediate supervisor, whereas other background details relating to salary, etc, can be communicated by the librarian, deputy or personnel assistant. Such division of responsibility for communication during induction is followed at the Library of New South Wales in the following manner:

'The new employee is first welcomed and interviewed by the training librarian, or if he is not a professional officer, by the administrative assistant. At this point he is given, among other leaflets, one entitled *Your introduction to the Library of New South Wales* and another, *Your introduction to the . . . Department.* In most cases he is then introduced to the deputy principal librarian who signs his library identification card. He then goes to the staff clerk who supplies him with information on public service regulations and internal library regulations and general orders, on salary and salary progressions, and similar routine matters, and then introduces him to the head of the department in which he will be working and to his immediate supervisor within that department. The " supervisor " conducts a follow-up interview ten days later, and in the second month of the employment a joint interview is held by the training librarian and the administrative assistant. A detailed *Induction and action* form to be filled in at the appropriate stages ensures that all necessary action is taken from the issue of a dozen or so leaflets on a variety of topics to an ultimate recommendation for permanent appointment ' (McGreal 48).

This example helps to spotlight another factor relating to induction, namely its timing and length. Much information will obviously be communicated during the first few days of employment. So far as these first few days are concerned, opinions differ as to whether the new member of staff should be introduced primarily to the department in which he will be working or to the library as a whole. Many libraries (*eg* Bradford University Library) plan visits to each of the library departments for their new staff in their first few days but other libraries (*eg* Coventry Public Library) prefer the reverse practice of allowing staff to settle into the department in which they are to work and then introducing them to other departments during subsequent week(s). The latter system is to be favoured for junior staff, since it attempts to avoid confusion resulting from the presentation of too much information and too many new surroundngs immediately a person starts work in the library. The first process is to be favoured for senior staff since often their departmental duties and responsibilities need to be learnt and judged in relation to library service and concepts as a whole.

Delayed induction to the library as a whole may result from other factors than the wish to avoid confusion in the first few days. It may be more convenient to hold an induction course once or twice a year. This can then be planned for a time convenient to senior staff and supervisors and can facilitate the grouping together of a number of new entrants. Durham University Library, for example, holds an induction course for new staff in the Christmas vacation, this course including talks, discussions and visits to sections of the library and to other libraries.

Secondly, the induction course might be one planned by a university or local government authority for new employees of the wider organisation. Staffordshire County Library, for example, runs an induction course for newly appointed junior staff. This is held annually on one day a week for thirteen weeks. Half the day is spent on a county council induction course conducted by the county council training officers and the other half consists of talks and discussions on aspects of the library service by senior members of library staff, followed (for staff from branches) by a period of practical work in one of the departments of hq. A similar scheme operates in Surrey where the library trainees attend a Surrey County Council course for new local government entrants. This course introduces entrants to the organisation and functions of local authorities and provides an opportunity of testing independently in discussion and written work each new entrant's aptitudes and ability for service in local government.

The close link between induction and training in such arrangements is obvious. There is no clear dividing line between the two, although if the course includes the imparting of skills over a period of time and the testing of aptitudes, then it may well be more accurate to speak of this as training rather than induction. Induction may be phased over a period of weeks but in theory and practice does not usually (unless delayed) extend more than two months; after this period any introduction to library departments or service usually displays characteristics of training.

One difference of approach to staff induction, which is usually evident within any one particular library, relates to the distinction between junior and senior staff. Many libraries have a more elaborate system of library induction for new seniors, juniors receiving limited departmental induction. This is justified by such arguments as ' a junior's duties usually require him or her to know less of the workings of other departments and the library in general than a senior's duties require'. Furthermore, induction for juniors may be linked more closely to training and periodic rotation.

On the other hand, some libraries organise library-wide induction courses for new junior staff but not seniors. Such libraries include Essex University Library and Edinburgh University Library. Presumably, one of the main arguments in favour of this arrangement is that senior staff have a greater awareness of librarianship and the library in which they are newly employed and will pick up more background information as a result of their day-to-day activities than is the case with juniors. This argument has its merits but is rather tenuous if it seeks to maintain that senior staff do not need an induction course. Should a person be promoted within the library, induction might be cut or shortened. Thus in Camden Libraries ' new ' senior staff are normally Camden trainees, already familiar with the system; hence on return from library school they are given just a short re-orientation course, which includes meetings with the director, deputies, principal assistant and appropriate heads of departments. Otherwise, however, if these special circumstances do not apply, induction appears advisable for all new staff.

A small library may adopt a very informal approach to induction, with the librarian introducing new staff to the system as a whole, then handing them over to relevant heads of departments. In most libraries, however, there are advantages to be gained from adopting a more formal approach. This will facilitate decisions relating to the best person to supervise or undertake a particular part of the induction course, the aims of the course, its precise content and so on. Information which it is thought the new member of staff should obtain may be listed on a form, indicating when the information is to be communicated. Such a check list, based on an idea presented in *Induction* by R Van Gelder (pages 8-9), is given here.

120

Category of information	Timing		
	Pre-Employment	First Day	First 4/8 weeks
1 EMPLOYMENT CONDITIONS			
Remuneration	✓		
Method of payment (how, where, when)		✓	
Hours of work	✓		
Overtime (frequency and payment)			✓
Holidays	✓		
Sickness payment	✓		
Superannuation	✓		
Probationary period			✓
2 PROCEDURES			
Explanation of salary slip			✓
Time recording and keeping		✓	
Absence			✓
Certification requirements			✓
Telephone calls			✓
3 HEALTH, SAFETY & WELFARE			
Medical examination	✓		
First aid regulations and facilities		✓	
Fire precautions			✓
Smoking		✓	
Staff room and canteens		✓	
Recreation facilities			✓
4 STAFF RELATIONS, RESPONSIBILITIES & DEVELOPMENT			
Initial assignment	✓	✓	
Name of supervisor		✓	
Duties and job responsibilities	✓		✓
Library organisation			✓
Education and training	✓		✓
Transfer and promotion prospects	✓		✓
5 RELATED ORGANISATIONS			
Professional (LA etc)			✓
Trade union			✓
Social club/staff guild			✓

Fig 3 INDUCTION CHECK LIST

The ticks in the list indicate possible timings in a typical situation but obviously circumstances will differ with each library. When ticks for the same subject appear in two columns they indicate a brief outline, say, prior to employment, with a more detailed explanation later on. The check list may be modified to indicate who is to communicate what and by what means (spoken or written). A check list with this type of detail is used by the Library of New South Wales and was referred to in a quotation presented above.

Training
Besides aiming at the imparting of information over a period of time and testing aptitudes for work, training is distinguished from induction by the fact that it seeks to impart skills; not only information relating to such skills but their actual employment and experience. Hence there is more emphasis on participation, learning by doing, rather than merely being informed. Training, like communication to which it is closely linked, is a continuous process. J Paerdee has stated in relation to the North Central Regional Library, Wenatchee, Washington: 'The regional library trains when it hires, trains when it orients, trains during every communication, trains during every staff workshop and every branch visit, and counts the job never done' (Paerdee 357). Such a view, seeing training involved in numerous activities and by various means, is a more realistic one than that which sees training as being confined to a formal oral programme for junior professional trainees.

In examining the training that takes place during day-to-day supervision or staff meetings, the librarian or senior administrator will, in effect, be examining the nature and efficiency of general library management and communication. In such instances the aims of training will be linked to the aims of management. If it is decided that other types of training should be examined, instituted or reshaped in a more formal manner, as with so many other instances of managerial investigation and decision making, some definition should be given to the need for formal training schemes, to the objectives and expected results, and methods to be employed. Such definition should be related to available resources (financial, human and physical) and the attempt made to evaluate the success of the training programme.

The general aim of any training programme will be to create

conditions in which people are able to learn most effectively and apply their learning in library service. It involves the imparting and application of information and somewhat intangible qualities such as judgement and enthusiasm. Its content and methods will obviously vary according to the size of the library, type of staff involved (*eg* non-professional), plus factors mentioned above such as precise objectives and available resources. A more detailed listing of objectives, against which local needs and resources may be set, is presented by INTAMEL (Intamel 261):

Objectives
Increasing efficiency / performance
Integration of individuals for greater unity
Increasing interest and making individuals and service more effective
Familiarization with objectives and principles
Familiarization with resources
Familiarization with routine processes
Increasing job satisfaction
Imparting professional and general knowledge
Safeguarding the quality of the service
Preparing for specific jobs in the organization
Preparing for promotion
Improving staff morale
Increasing spirit of co-operation
To develop qualities of leadership
To impart knowledge of management techniques
To prepare personnel for supervisory roles.

Such a listing clearly indicates that the aims are on various levels: firstly, to teach a particular job and its related skills, secondly, to communicate conceptions of library goals and thirdly, to develop motivation in the trainee for accomplishing his tasks as efficiently as possible.

The types of training offered by individual libraries vary tremendously. W R Van Dersal identifies four types of training for organisations in general:

1 orientive training
2 job or production training
3 maintenance or refresher course
4 career or developmental training (Van Dersal 100).

Van Dersal acknowledges that these four types merge freely into one another. Cumberland County Library's approach to staff development comprises induction (which would roughly correspond to Van Dersal's first point) and three elements of training:

1 ' on the job ' training
2 formal training lectures
3 training and re-training of senior staff (*eg* by weekend courses).

Both Van Dersal's listing and that relating to Cumberland contain elements of classification by type of staff (*eg* professional trainees —career or development training; training and re-training of senior staff) and by method employed (*eg* ' on the job ' training). Such a cross classification is inevitable since some methods (*eg* formal training programmes) are often aimed at particular categories of staff (in this example perhaps professional trainees), while other methods (*eg* ' on the job ' training) can be provided for all staff save the most senior of new appointments.

P B Smith describes four ways in which an organisation can attempt to train its staff:

1 dispense with the need to attempt training by hiring an alternative, more skilled, man in place of the first
2 train a man for taking more responsibility by appointing him to it right away
3 attempt to instruct him inside the actual situation in which he works
4 make use of some specialised training facility. This may be within the organisation in the case of a personnel or training department; it may be a service provided by a firm of consultants or an industry staff college, or it may be a specific course at a university or technical college (Smith 274-5).

Libraries tend to use all four methods. American libraries display a more marked tendency than British libraries to follow a policy of promotion from within but promotion from within is partly a function of size, larger systems obviously having more persons to chose from for particular appointments. Except for the very top jobs, promotion from within has always occurred in very large provincial public libraries; in London, since 1965, there has been a marked increase in internal promotion. Smaller systems will be more likely to recruit new staff for senior posts. The second method, which would utilise the old maxim of ' learning by one's mistakes ', may be necessary in a library unable to devote resources to training but it is not particularly satisfactory since it could involve a lowering of standards of efficiency relating to library service. The third method of learning 'on the job' is widely used in libraries. One disadvantage of this method may be that the trainee gets a limited view of the library's work and that the supervisor's own work suffers through having to pay constant attention to the trainee. Hence it is desirable to combine 'on the job' training with more formal facilities, as indicated in Smith's fourth method.

Numerous accounts of training programmes in libraries, indicating the types of programmes held and categories of staff at which they are aimed, exist in published literature (*eg* Dudley Public Library—Dean; Library of New South Wales—McGreal; Library of Congress—*Training programs at LC*). The account of training at the Library of Congress, in particular, describes the wide variety of training for staff with varying levels of duty and experience, avoiding undue emphasis on professional trainees. An example of a detailed account of a programme for professional trainees is Surrey County Library's *Scheme for trainee librarians*.

One final important point relating to training and communication is that the library should communicate about its training programme as well as during the training itself. As already indicated, training is closely linked to communication, much training being achieved through communication. Furthermore, communication is used to record and assess training. Leeds City Libraries, for example, maintain detailed records of their training programme for library assistants. These records include a listing of all items or aspects of service that an assistant is to be taught in a particular department, the person responsible for training indicating against items on this list the date on which training started and the date on which competence in the task was achieved (City of Leeds).

Libraries should also communicate about their training, in the sense that staff involved (trainers and trainees) are given clear indications of the purpose and nature of the training and how it will be evaluated. A person learns only when he is motivated to do so and not simply through processes of repetitive practice or exposure. Communication about training, its purpose, its progress and evaluation, will help provide motivation and interest necessary in any training and also help focus attention on the efficiency of the training.

5

The dividing line between many interviews and day-to-day discussions is very blurred. A discussion, such as that arising when a librarian calls the superintendent of branch libraries into his office to consider future branch development, shares many characteristics with the more formal type of interview, say, an employment interview. There will be an exchange of information and ideas; the librarian will inform the branch superintendent as to what sort of development seems feasible and will relate this to impressions of what the branch superintendent and his staff think and are capable of doing. Throughout the discussion both persons should be seeking to maintain a sense of cooperative effort and enthusiasm. The relationship between participants in a discussion or an interview, in fact, is an important determinant of the effectiveness of the communication between them. Considerations relating to effect discussed in a previous chapter apply in all forms of contact. So too do considerations relating to oral and written communication, interviews usually combining the two means. An employment interview, for example, could in large measure be based on a written application form, the interviewer getting the candidate to expand on and explain certain points. In such oral contact the interviewer has the communication advantage of gaining factual information and attitudes in a face-to-face setting.

Attention here is focused on meetings which are normally thought of and described in terms of ' interviews ', as opposed to less formal day-to-day discussions.

a) Employment interview

The employment type of interview bears one disadvantage which is not present in other types such as appraisal interviews. This disadvantage is that the interviewer(s) does not usually know the candidate, does not know very much about his personality, his attitudes and capabilities other than may be deduced from written statements of such qualities provided in references. This makes it particularly difficult to fulfil what is really the aim of all selection, namely to predict the candidate's behaviour in some future context: to predict whether he will fit into a certain staff situation and be capable of fulfilling certain expected functions. The circumstances surrounding this difficulty are also conditioned by a further factor, which only adds to the initial difficulty. This factor is that the interview is an artificial, as opposed to a natural, every-day working situation. The candidate does not necessarily demonstrate his usual approach to problems because of nervousness or inability to give an adequate acount of himself and obviously this complicates the interviewer's task of assessing his potential behaviour and capabilities.

The most that the interviewer can do to overcome this difficulty, to attempt to promote a normal and meaningful oral encounter, is to pay attention to the quality of the interview. This process involves precisely defining the purpose of the interview and attempting to fulfil these purposes by skilled technique or method. As in other communication situations, the experience of the interviewer and maturity of the candidate affects the success of the interview.

Any interviewer must carefully consider and define the purposes of the interview he is to conduct. If he fails to do this he may well be uncertain as to what information or impressions he requires of the candidate and may not be very helpful in providing the candidate himself with information about the job. There are three basic purposes of an employment interview:

1 to obtain all relevant information from the candidate as to his capabilities, experience and general attitudes, in order to be able to assess his suitability for the job

2 to give the candidate the clearest possible picture of the job and what will be required in that job. Certain types of preliminary information involved here were indicated above in a discussion of induction. The interviewer has a responsibility to be as frank and as helpful as possible in pursuing this aim; he should not attempt to gloss over disadvantages relating to the job

3 to treat the candidate with professional and personal courtesy. This involves replying promptly and helpfully to his pre-interview enquiries and being as considerate and as friendly as possible on the day of the interview. By acting in this way the interviewer or personnel officer is helping the candidate to form impressions of the library (it is to be hoped that attitudes displayed to candidates are a true reflection of the library's constant concern for its staff) and helping to put the candidate at ease, thus facilitating his interview performance. Conversely, of course, the candidate has a responsibility to the library to treat its invitation with courtesy and accord questions truth and frankness.

Much information relating to a candidate will be obtained before the interview on a written application form. Similarly, much information about the library and the job will be obtained by the candidate before the interview. Often this is left to the candidate's own initiative, to use his personal contacts and printed sources such as annual reports. Where possible, however, the library should assist such an accumulation of information by sending the candidate a job analysis before the interview or carefully going over such an analysis at the interview.

The interviewer has more likelihood of obtaining required information if he prepares some sort of check list before the interview takes place. This should not result in a stereotyped set of questions but should provide the interviewer with a guide to getting information he needs for assessing the candidate.

Many libraries used printed forms of questions to guide interviewers (*eg* in Herts County, forms list points relating to qualifications, relevant experience, knowledge and use of books and libraries, hobbies, health, hours to be worked and salary, appearance and manner, etc. Slightly different printed forms are used for hq and divisional interviews). Even if a library does not use such a form it is usual for a library interview, for any post, to be structured in the sense that a particular pattern of questions is adhered to. The advantage of using the structured interview is that it reduces unreliability by conditioning what information is sought. In turn the structured interview should help condition the evaluation of the information and hence how the candidate is assessed. In so doing it can help eliminate personal bias which the interviewer may have or develop toward the candidate. In short, the structured interview provides a greater potentiality (not an absolute guarantee) of reliability and validity.

The unstructured interview, in contrast, ' is one in which the pattern of questions, the circumstances under which these questions are asked and the bases for evaluation of replies to these questions are not standardised. These factors vary from one interview to another and from one applicant to another. In short, the unstructured interview is subjective in the extreme. This subjectivity may lead different interviewers to disagree quite markedly about the suitability of a particular applicant. Such disagreement adversely affects both the reliability and validity of unstructured interviews ' (Siegel 114).

Library interviews are normally structured in another sense

apart from the pattern of questions. The interviewer or panel, which is usual for senior or graded posts, is normally the same for particular types of job interviews. A panel interview may have the advantages of eliminating individual interviewer bias and of questioning the candidate more thoroughly and precisely than would otherwise be possible. The panel type of interview does, however, also possess some disadvantages. It may lead to repetitive and confused, rather than thorough, questioning. This disadvantage may perhaps be overcome by the panel meeting before the interview to discuss the job specification, to ensure that they have a common and adequate knowledge of the job involved and to work out a common attitude to the type of person they are seeking for the post. A further disadvantage of the panel interview is that it is less easy to establish rapport with the applicant, even though members of the panel may be introduced individually to the candidate. In general, it may be said that while the most useful and complete information is likely to be gathered by a single interviewer, provided he is skilled and experienced, the panel method helps compensate for lack of individual interviewing skill and is possibly fairer to the applicant. Furthermore, the panel interview allows various organisational elements or interests (*eg* in the case of a public library—the library, local authority, and public representatives) to be represented and hence is almost inevitable in senior library appointments.

The check list of information required and hence of questions to be asked at the interview is, in its most sophisticated form, a job specification, providing a guide to estimating the abilities of the person whom it is thought would perform the job successfully. Such a specification is based on a job analysis, an analysis of the duties involved in a job. The analysis should contain adequate detail and accurate information and may be sent to the candidates before the interview. Typical elements of job analysis are:

1 job title

2 grade

3 wage or salary range

4 brief description of duties (including a note of how frequently they are performed)

5 social aspects of the job (gregarious/solitary; supervision; persuasion)

6 responsibilities

i Cash, methods, planning, records, materials, equipment

ii Personal

7 working conditions

i Physical conditions

ii Hours (normal, overtime, shift)

iii Holidays

iv Privileges, concessions, etc.

8 prospects (Sidney & Brown 70).

This information, of use to the candidate and the employers, is then translated by the employer into a job specification, in order to relate estimates of ability and performance to the job elements. The specification is not entirely composed of estimates or assessments. Some of the information is of a factual nature (*eg* personal data, such as age and home circumstances) and can be obtained by consulting a candidate's certificates and forms, that is by more objective methods than questioning at the interview itself, when the candidate might give the wrong information or withhold certain facts. Other elements of the specification, however, are subject to estimate and assessment. The method of obtaining facts may not be one hundred percent objective (*ie* may rely on what the candidate says alone) and these facts may form the basis of assessment. Thus the interviewer may seek details of spare-time activities and from the information given him by the candidate relate this to the job by forming an assessment of his social roles, his ability to get on with people and supervise others.

It will be appreciated that such processes are subject to a lack of complete objectivity in gaining information from the candidate and also to a possible inaccurate or misguided assessment of the information by the interviewer relating the information to the job. Such misguided assessment may be made in error or may be the result of biased attitudes or impressions, as when an interviewer misinterprets verbal fluency as being a sign of intelligence. Even more tenuous will be the interviewer's attempt to gain some insight into the candidate's future aspirations and goals, since here even the candidate is not in the main describing facts, which may be objectively collected and checked, but ideas and assessments of his own capabilities and jobs. The interviewer in turn relates his own perceptions of the candidate and job to the perceptions of the candidate himself. The complete process may result in a lack of valid assessment of candidate in relation to job.

These are disadvantages which must be accepted. The assessment of a junior for a particular post may largely involve the collection of factual information by objective methods. For more senior posts, however, it is necessary and desirable to obtain some assessment of a candidate's personality and his potential ability in a particular job. Inevitably the assessment will be far from perfect but, providing the interviewer is reasonably skilled and follows a tested and structured form of interview, the percentage error will be considerably reduced.

A number of standard or specimen job specifications exist. As an example, one may cite that formulated and tested over a number of years by Elizabeth Sidney and Margaret Brown. Their list, which is itself an adaptation of the seven point plan of the National Institute of Industrial Psychology (Rodger), lists items of factual data under the headings 1 personal data, *eg* age and sex, 2 physique, 3 educational and technical qualifications and training, 4 work or other experience, and indications of abilities required under 5 mental abilities, 6 social roles, 7 initiative, 8 emotional stability and 9 motivation (Sidney & Brown 55-56).

In utilising such a specification the interviewer may give the candidate a graded assessment (A, B, C, etc) against each element or may make more detailed written comments. Where possible, the writing of such comments should not intrude upon the oral conduct of the interview. The technique employed by the interviewer should have as its most important variable the attempt to put the candidate at ease and to get him to do most of the talking. Both these occurrences depend on the interviewer displaying a friendly attitude, a genuine interest in what the candidate has to say and the ability to listen effectively and sympathetically. Such ability requires attention and is not facilitated by the interviewer writing incessantly when the candidate is talking.

b) Appraisal interview

The appraisal interview often bears similar characteristics as that part of an employment interview which attempts to assess the personality of a candidate and predict his behaviour in certain future situations. This similarity is particularly evident if the assessment interview attempts not merely to review a person's work and progress in, say, the past year—that is to make potentially objective observations on actual happenings—but to plan a future programme of work and progress in relation to a particular personality. In the latter case job specifications, such as the National Institute of Industrial Psychology's seven point plan or its modification produced by Sidney and Brown, may well be used as they are in employment interviews.

As was seen in the above discussion of the employment interview, assessment can be a hazardous task for the unskilled assessor and, since it may relate to personality traits and perceptions of possible or theoretical work and events, lacks objectivity in varying degrees. For this reason appraisals have been subject to much criticism. A two year DSIR project supervised by Professor Norman C Hunt into how appraisals procedures worked in six firms, for example, revealed that appraisers are reluctant to appraise and that their assessments displayed the 'skewed tendency', the tendency to award average or above average marks in any rating scale used (Rowe. See also McGregor, 1957).

Most criticism is directed against appraisal which judges a person in terms of personality traits such as mental alertness, integrity, adaptability, job interest and so on. It is difficult to conduct such a judgement or appraisal since it is hard to identify relevant factors in the personality and relate them to success at work. The criteria to be used by the assessor are often hard to define or explain and assessors vary substantially in their capacity to judge people. Judgements are therefore likely to be subjective and lack uniformity. Examples of rating forms used in this type of appraisal include the *Personnel services rating report* published by the American Library Association, Library Administration Division. It covers thirty four factors, rated on a four point scale, and is heavily oriented toward personality traits such as judgement, self-confidence, quality of work, cooperativeness, etc.

This type of rating is often motivated by the necessity of evaluating a person in order to justify salary increments or increases, or promotion. In the Library of New South Wales, heads of departments and, in some cases, immediate supervisors, report on officers under their control at a time when they become eligible for an increment or for promotion. If the reporting officer makes an adverse report on an officer he is required to discuss it with the deputy principal librarian before showing his report to the officer reported on. The report has to be shown to the person reported on in each case and signed by him as evidence that he has seen it and also given the opportunity to make his comments on the report (McGreal 58).

The reporting system in the Library of New South Wales is also motivated by the fact that it is a fairly large library and it is felt necessary to keep in contact, by some form of regular reporting, with officers after they have passed the periods at which they receive formal in-service training. This factor of size of staff partly helps to explain the more widespread use of rating forms in American libraries than in their British counterparts (Peele 69). An additional reason is that American public libraries have a responsibility for administration that is held in Britain by the local government establishment officer. In British libraries the only form of assessment employed is often a departmental head report and/or an interview with the librarian or other senior officer for trainees or new staff, on completion of a probationary period of employment. At Bradford University Library, for example, all junior staff are appointed first on a temporary basis; before becoming permanent they are assessed by their head of department and usually interviewed by the deputy librarian.

This type of assessment or appraisal interview will have more success in relation to purposes (discussed below) if objective standards are used as far as possible. To ensure effective communication at an assessment interview it is necessary to ensure that supervisor and subordinate are both starting from the same job analysis or specification. It often happens that the reality of the job is different from its description or analysis on paper, partly because people tend to modify their jobs to fit their own strengths and interests. Therefore, if a written form must be used, items requiring personality judgements should be eliminated as far as possible and only objective standards used. That is to say, job description and work performed should be emphasised rather than whether a person is of neat appearance and displays self-confidence. A discussion of job and performance is more likely to motivate a person toward additional or improved performances, whereas a personality traits rating is likely to arouse his hostility and self-defence mechanisms and hence lead to ineffective communication. The traits method often centres on a discussion of a person's faults or shortcomings; such an approach usually inhibits open discussion and change in that person.

5*

The rating method of assessment, using formal assessment criteria, be they related to personality or performance, has more relevance for junior and perhaps new senior staff than to senior staff during their management development. It is useful to have a report on new staff, to show their fitness for library employment or work in a particular post and how they have responded to library induction and training. This method is not so relevant to assessment on the management development side. As a result, libraries which do use staff appraisal and give attention to all staff in such processes, not just new juniors, tend to use more informal methods of assessing heads of departments or sections and, possibly, other senior staff as well. The rating form, or printed list of criteria, is dispensed with and a more flexible approach made to task attainment and personnel development. This approach involves as much discussion and self-awareness of development as mere assessment by the superior. As such it has much relevance to the goals method of appraisal discussed below.

An appraisal interview is an exercise in staff communication and concern with its effectiveness has led many commentators to advocate, and some industrial companies to follow, the goals method (DeProspero) with emphasis on job related performance, rather than the personality traits method. Deriving much from Peter Drucker's concept of management by objectives, the goals approach emphasises analysis rather than appraisal, implying a more positive and objective approach. The procedure consists of the superior and subordinate identifying key areas of the subordinate's job and then deciding what level of achievement in each of these areas would represent a satisfactory result. Attention is often directed to the question of what conditions one could expect to see if the job was being done well, discussion of this question helping the identification of key results which the employee should be aiming at. The procedure is usually accomplished largely by oral discussion. Sometimes supervisor and subordinate prepare notes beforehand to aid discussion. Similarly, it is useful to have a written summary of oral discussion; this may be prepared by the superior or by the two persons jointly.

This goals approach has certain advantages. There is less of a tendency for personality to become an issue. The emphasis is on the future rather than the past, aiming at the establishment of realistic targets and seeking the most effective ways of reaching them. Thus appraisal becomes a means for a constructive end, the end of performance related to concrete goals within a particular time setting, say, six months. Since the member of staff plays a major rather than an insignificant or subordinate part in setting these goals of the job and determining the means by which progress can be measured, greater staff enthusiasm and compliance should be assured and more effective communication obtained. Above all, unless the system becomes routine and loses its attraction, this method of appraisal, this exercise in staff communication, will contribute more to the ends of individual staff development and performance and hence library service.

One English librarian who holds annual appraisal interviews with his departmental and sectional heads sees these interviews as ' an essential part of our communication system which in turn is intended to promote a real spirit of participative management and a sense of personal accountability for results '. In addition, he seeks to ensure that these department and sectional heads are undertaking similar interviews, albeit in varying forms ranging from discussion to the ' occasional word ', with their own subordinates.

In seeking to identify the purposes of the appraisal interview, it should be emphasised that to attempt to achieve too many purposes may be confusing and unhelpful, since individual purpose (*eg* rating for promotional purposes; goal setting) may well require a different approach and be individually time-consuming. The basic aim of the appraisal interview, conducted according to the goals method and applicable to most levels of staff, should be to make the best use of staff in the library. This may involve some discussion of past achievements, some downward communication as to where a member of staff stands and the recognition of his good work, but the main content should be oriented to future performance. This will involve much upward communication and self-appraisal on the part of the subordinate.

Any exercise in communication or aspect of communication and staff management is, or should be, linked to numerous other aspects within the whole context of staff communication and management. Job appraisal is linked, in a time sequence, to employment interviews. Many organisations tend to concentrate on selection procedures and then fail to make the best use of staff so carefully selected. Appraisals are ' part of the career development programme which will increasingly allow a closer match between the interests and abilities of the individual officer and the needs of the organisation, so that an officer is placed in a job to which he is well fitted ' (GB Civil Service Dept 4).

Appraisal itself should not be an event in isolation. It requires adequate follow-up and feed-back discussion of actual performance in relation to established goals and hence repetition at regular intervals, say, every six or twelve months. Furthermore, it needs to be linked to other elements of communication and management such as staff training. Finally, of course, since effective performance depends only partly on personal attributes and enthusiasm but also on the attributes of colleagues and relations with them, library management must carefully link individual appraisals in order to link persons and their organisation within the library to general library goals.

c) Grievance interview and counselling

One difficulty involved in any communication, one factor which inhibits effective communication, is that it is often hard or impossible for both sender and receiver to understand the matter or situation in terms of the same frame of reference. This problem is particularly acute in grievance interviews or counselling, since one person's attention and thoughts are focused on a particular situation which is causing him disturbance. In order to be able to communicate effectively, the receiver must take steps to understand the situation and the sender's view of it as fully as possible.

Grievance interviews usually involve some form of counselling, that is working through a person's problem and possibly suggesting solutions for it. For this reason the two types of interview have been linked in this section. Both types often overlap with a third, namely the discipline interview, at which the person being disciplined may give vent to grievances and require advice.

Only the largest of libraries make special arrangements for grievance interviews or staff counselling. In the Library of Congress, for example, the Employee Relations Office handles a considerable diversity of job related problems. These include communication, on the job relations, misunderstandings of Library of Congress policies and procedures, leave, lack of recognition, performance ratings and dissatisfaction with current positions. In the fiscal year 1972 employee counselling included 5,858 interviews. Of these 3,256 were job related, 1,486 were for financial counselling, 600 for personal problems and the remaining categories of domestic, leave and health-related made up the difference (*Libr of Congress Info Bull,* 31 (39) Sept 29 1972 424).

Like other libraries, the Library of Congress encourages the initial discussion of problems with supervisors. The primary objective of the Employee Relation's Office is ' to assist supervisors and employees in their efforts to establish and maintain relationships which make working together a satisfying and productive experience ' (*Libr of Congress Info Bull,* 31 (13) March 31 1972 1). This encouragement is often stated in staff procedural manuals. For example, a paragraph on grievances from the Detroit Public Library staff handbook reads as follows :

' When you have a grievance—something that you think is not right in your work or work situation—talk it over first with your agency head and see if he can satisfactorily take care of the problem. The reason for this is easy to see : your agency head is closest to your work and the conditions under which you work, and in many cases he has the necessary authority to make adjustments. Occasionally, however, situations do arise that cannot be handled by the agency head. In such cases you are invited to consult with other members of the administrative staff—usually your service director or the personnel director. Then, if the problem is still unresolved, you may feel free to ask for an appointment to see the director ' (page 19).

In most libraries, smaller than the Library of Congress, such procedures are normally followed in an informal manner, especially the discussion of problems with immediate supervisor or head of department. Yet whatever the frequency and formality of this type of interview, the person conducting the interview or informal discussion should still pay attention to its communication aspects. It is particularly important that the interviewer or receiver should pay attention to the act of listening. He must give the person before him time and encouragement to state his case as fully as possible; his attitude should display willingness to listen, sympathy for the speaker's point of view and problems. Employee cases, grievances or problems, may be presented in an emotional manner and the listener should endeavour to communicate his feelings of sympathy, not necessarily in words, but often through non-verbal means such as nods of interest.

In some situations the supervisor or librarian's ability to listen may be almost all that is required. The member of staff may well work out a solution to his own problem as he talks, with occasional interjections from the supervisor, through a release of emotion and and a restatement of facts bearing on the case. In this type of non-directive counselling the supervisor does not argue or attempt to discipline the employee but hears his case and then uses the information so presented to try to help dispel anxieties. Such counselling obviously requires a lot of patience and emotional stability on the part of the counsellor.

Directive counselling, discipline type interviews, or grievance interviews in which the person complaining may be at fault, involve continuous two way dialogue. Through such dialogue the supervisor attempts to get all facts relevant to a situation, facts which will enable him to make a pronouncement on the situation. The term ' situation ' is stressed here. Although particular attention must be paid to a person's feelings, it is easier to view a situation, to make a judgement on this in objective terms, than it is to view and judge behaviour surrounding the situation. For example, it is easier to analyse the divisions of work and responsibilities within a department than the behaviour relating to such a division, which might have caused staff arguments. An understanding of the situation should give the supervisor a greater and more accurate insight into a dispute than the mere examination of staff behaviour. Such an analysis of the situation in factual terms with the employee often enables apparent deadlock in attitudes or argument to be broken and a move made toward a settlement of the problem.

Some form of follow-up is often necessary from a grievance or counselling interview. One of the most obvious would be a second interview, at which the discussion of a problem is continued or at which the supervisor presents his case or solution in the light of investigations he has conducted between the two interviews. Another type of follow-up is for the supervisor to discuss the matter raised by a member of staff with that person's immediate head or other relevant person. Such a follow-up, however, involves the matter of confidences. The supervisor or interviewer must obviously treat a matter as confidential should the employee request or stipulate this. The Library of Congress Employee Relations Office, for example, will seek to establish communication between two parties, say, a supervisor and employee with differences, if desired by the consultant; otherwise interviews and counselling sessions are strictly confidential.

It may be possible and desirable for the interviewer to take follow-up measures, such as altering administrative arrangements or divisions of staff responsibilities which led to a dispute, without revealing that a member of staff had complained or been to see him. Where it is necessary to make such a revelation this should be preceded by a request for the employee's permission so that a confidence may not be broken. Often the employee will leave the interviewer with a blanket permission to investigate the problem and take action as deemed necessary; in such situations the employee is mainly concerned to present his case and hopes that some alleviation may follow. If this is so, part of the interviewer's follow-up should always be to keep the employee personally informed as to actions taken which have resulted from the original interview or discussion. This informing is not simply a matter of courtesy but also a recognition of the fact that grievance interviews and counselling are part of the process by which an organisation is made to work and be subject to development, and that such processes should be communicated to all relevant members of staff.

d) Exit interview

An exit interview, more usually held in commercial and industrial companies than in libraries, is often associated in such companies with employee dismissal. In libraries, employees are rarely dismissed. A new junior entrant from school might be advised, after a probationary period, that he or she was not suited to library work and the suggestion made that the person resign. Similarly, a person's resignation might be requested following the discovery of irregularities in the fines money. Otherwise, most resignations are purely voluntary.

Although, however, the circumstances of departure might differ for library staff, an exit interview can still be of value. In many libraries the ' interview ' is quite informal. In Liverpool University Library, for example, the librarian attempts to see all staff who are leaving, just before their departure, for an informal chat. In many other libraries no such discussion takes place between the chief librarian and leaver, unless on the initiative of the leaver, but similar discussion may occur between the leaver and his head of department.

The exit interview, as conducted in libraries, is in part an exercise in public relations or professional courtesy. It is desirable that the junior leaving, going to take up other employment in the same town and forming part of the library's public clientele in the case of a public library, should leave with favourable impressions of the senior library staff, even if disillusionment with the work. It is desirable that a senior member of staff, moving to another library and hence still intimately involved in the library profession, should leave with similar impressions; this should be possible if the librarian's concern at a person's leaving mirrors his concern for staff while they are under his employment.

It is to be hoped that the reasons for a person leaving would have been discussed by the librarian or a senior member of staff well before that person's actual departure, say, when he submits his resignation or on the first intimation that this was forthcoming. Discussion at this stage might enable difficulties to be resolved, if such difficulties were to be the cause of an otherwise unwilling departure. A person might not, for example, be able to continue working in a particular department, due to a clash of personalities, or the work involved. If this becomes known the member of staff might be allocated duties in another department or alternative work and hence the ' difficulty ' resolved.

If such resolution of staff problems is undertaken in a library, discussion at exit interviews should, in the main, comprise general exchange of views on the library or particular departments, possibly going into some detail of particular aspects of departmental work. In other words, although a person may not be leaving because of difficulties or dissatisfactions encountered but simply for self-advancement, he may nevertheless be able to express opinions of some use to the librarian. Due to the person's impending departure, the expression of such opinions may be freer than would have been the case at an earlier stage in his employment. The librarian may with advantage note actual or implied criticism of working conditions, administrative efficiency or staff relations and later take steps to investigate such situations for himself. As in other types of interview, communication is aided by a willingness on the part of the more senior member of staff to listen patiently and attempt to ensure that the exchange is as free and as frank as possible. If the exchange has revealed or stimulated any useful ideas or knowledge, the librarian may with advantage make written notes once the exit interview has finished and follow this up with further staff discussions and action.

CHAPTER SEVEN

Aids and hindrances

NON-RECEIPT or misunderstanding of transmitted messages or data, occurrences often emphasised in discussion of personal, internal organisational and mass communication, are not the only hindrances to effective communication. Aids and hindrances to communication can be considered in relation to three main categories, namely organisational, personal and physical. Discussion of a fourth category, linguistic aids and hindrances, has been presented in preceding chapters on process and means of communication. Organisational aids and hindrances relate to administrative arrangements, such as the division of staff with varying degrees of responsibility and authority and the provision of administrative channels and rules concerning formal staff communication. Personal aids and hindrances relate to individual and group attitudes and competence. Physical aids and hindrances concern physical working conditions, involving perhaps the erection of communication barriers by physical separation of working personnel and geographic separation of units of the library, as witnessed in any library possessing branch or departmental libraries.

Organisational
An ineffective flow of communication between senior administrative librarians and other staff may be basically the result of the organisational structure of the library. This structure is important since it may help to determine the level of personal or psychological barriers erected to staff communication; the sensible arrangement of staff and provision of formal communication channels or facilities may motivate good or adequate communication, whereas illogical arrangements and stunted communication channels may tend to exaggerate personal and group attitudes, which in turn mitigate against communication and staff cohesion. Although more important barriers to communication may relate to language and

behaviour, such factors operate within, and to some extent are conditioned by, organisational arrangements.

As seen in the chapter on organisational structure and communication, structural conditions may work to the disadvantage of good staff communication. A library with an exaggerated horizontal adminstrative structure and lines of command may well find that the necessary flow of orders and information from the librarian and deputy to the remaining staff and the upward transmission of information and opinions to the librarian and deputy is sluggish, even though interdepartmental communication may be excellent. Similarly, looking at organisational structure from the view of the individual departments, a large department with an unrealistic span of control may create barriers to communication within the department and between that and other departments of the library.

Clear organisation, a prerequisite of good communication, relates not only to administrative structure but also to relationships within that structure. Thus responsibilities and lines of authority of staff working within a particular administrative structure, be it basically vertical or horizontal, must be clearly defined and announced. These definitions may start with job descriptions, indicating duties and responsibilities. Such job descriptions were formulated within Cumberland County Library a few years ago and have proved to be an invaluable aid, not only to the appointment of new staff, but also to general administration and staff cohesion.

One of the tried and tested principles of scientific management is the principle of authority, which stipulates that the lines of authority should be clearly defined. Nobody should be accountable to more than one supervisor, who must be held responsible for the acts of those subordinate to him. If, in addition, each member of staff knows his job through printed job descriptions and staff instructions, such persons should have clear understanding of their positions and bases for the pursuit of their activities. Such understanding or awareness will certainly not prevent the occurrence of communication and other staff difficulties but it should go a long way to removing personal uncertainty relating to work and areas of authority and responsibility.

Ease of communication and hence good communication is often associated with total size of the library. It is true that in a library with a small number of staff, relationships may be friendly and staff communication easy to conduct but it is a mistake to assume

142

that communications are bound to be good in the small system. The librarian in such a library may be on excellent social terms with his staff but still keep to himself information about the running of the library which he could with advantage share. The concern of C E N Childs, Librarian of Brunel University Library (staff size 28—Feb 1972), with communication, evident in his remark— ' The staff here is small and friendly and news travels fast; I sometimes think that I only have to think quietly in my office and within half an hour everybody knows '—is not necessarily repeated in all small libraries.

From the point of view of staff other than the librarian, the small library represents a simpler form of organisational and social system than does the larger system. There are fewer people, fewer levels in the organisational hierarchy and less minute sub-division of staff. It is easier for the employee to adapt himself to such a simpler system and to feel at ease within it. His work may become quickly meaningful to him because he can readily see its relation and importance to other functions and the organisation as a whole. In such a situation, closer relations should develop between the individual and the chief librarian and other senior members of the adminstrative staff, yet this is still no guarantee of good formal communication. Over-complexity of organisational structure is probably one of the most important and fundamental causes of poor staff relationships and communication, yet informality of relationships in the small system provides no guarantee that communication will be better than that existing in a large system whose subunits, staff responsibilities and communication channels are carefully defined and emphasised to all staff.

The growth in size of any library certainly brings with it administrative and communication problems. As the library increases in size it takes on special responsibilities (eg a public library might develop a hospital library or youth centre libraries). Furthermore, the staff become more numerous and are separated into more departments or assigned greater specialist functions. These parallel developments make it increasingly difficult for each member of staff to understand and relate to the various services and policies and to other individuals that affect him and his work. Division of work tends to make it easier to communicate within a comparatively small library department, since its members' activities are closely related and their physical location is likely to be close. Such division

143

does, however, increase the potential difficulties inherent in inter-departmental communication, simply because the number of depart-ments is increased and members of departments pursuing specialist activities may have less awareness of the activities and functions of staff in other departments than is the case in a smaller system. The specialisation, resultant from growth, complicates the exchange of information within a library.

Growth in size of a library results in another staff characteristic in addition to that of increased specialist activity. This is the employment of part-time and non-professional staff, who obviously differ in their tasks, their functions and perhaps their interests and attitudes, from full-time professional staff. These differences may be perpetuated by library arrangements, such as exclusion of non-professional staff from library staff meetings. Yet, whatever attempts senior professional staff make to involve non-professional staff in library activities and awareness of service, the outlook of these staff may well remain different. They may maintain different aware-ness of library services, administrative arrangements and communi-cation channels, simply through lack of general and professional education, and often create a further complexity to which com-munication arrangements must be adapted.

Similar comments apply to the employment of part-time staff. This is most evident in county systems. Thus, for example, the West Riding of Yorkshire County Library employs (March 1972) 302 full-time and 265 part-time non-manual staff. Glamorgan County Library employs (April 1972) 85 full-time and 42 part-time non-manual staff; the latter help to man 20 part-time branches, out of a total of 28 branch libraries. Even in smaller systems, however, part-time staff may form an important element of the total staff and affect communication. Thus in Dudley Public Library, with a total non-manual staff of 97 (March 1972), communication between the four full-time branches and central is better than between the part-time branches, which are manned by part-time staff who tend to have little contact with the central library except by telephone and memoranda (Dudley Public Library).

In such libraries, the challenge is obviously to create communica-tion systems which effectively compensate for communicative obstacles, often inherent in task specialisation and employee differentiation. This statement contains the assumption that the elimination of organisational barriers will eliminate organisation

144

communication problems. This, of course, is not true. As L O Thayer remarks, 'eliminating organisational barriers would be tantamount to eliminating the organisation itself' (Thayer, 1968 350). More complicated organisational arrangements and barriers are inevitable in a large system and must be accepted. If they are accepted in a constructive way, however, that is attention is given to overcoming difficulties inherent in them and preserving as good a formal communication system as is possible with the existing staff, then such a library may come to exhibit a sound organisational structure which, as stated above, may in turn help determine the level of personal barriers erected to staff communication.

Personalities and attitudes

A dilemma surrounds individual members of staff and the library as an organisation. It is necessary for the individual to identify himself with the library goals and work activities relating to library services so that he shall at least be sympathetic toward them and actively contribute toward their achievement as his duties demand. On the other hand, the individual is continually struggling to enhance his sense of self-esteem in relation to the organisation in which he works; the complete merger of his identity within any organisational structure may result in a gradual loss of personal identity and functions and hence of interest and sense of responsibility. Such a process of complete merger may be the result of personal attributes or deficiencies, such as an independent mind, but it can also result from, or be demanded in, libraries with low levels of personal responsibility below the librarian and deputy. This is a further illustration of the link between organisational and personal categories as described in this chapter. The allocation of realistic levels of responsibility and distribution of information can help promote a sense of individuality from which general library services will ultimately benefit.

Personal attributes or deficiencies are important since they can affect a communication system whatever its structure and attributes. Human behaviour in organisations is patterned, influenced by organisational circumstances, but personal characteristics can still produce a variety of behaviour in particular situations and under particular organisational arrangements. A person's capacity to communicate or capacity for understanding and hence receiving messages may simply be inadequate to the tasks he is expected to perform, to his job. As a result, he will create a communication barrier affecting not only himself but other persons related to him, other persons' work which is linked to his own. Recognition of capacity is the concern of employing authorities and senior administrative staff and the correct placement of a member of staff remains their responsibility. If bad performance is caused by simple ignorance or lack of information or instruction, this can be remedied and the person made fit for his present duties; if, however, he lacks innate capacity, he should be moved to a post whose duties are more commensurate with his abilities.

Other factors which may affect a person's work performance, his communication capacity and efficiency, relate to internal stress, prompted by, say, family or other personal worries and difficulties and temporary ill health. Since these factors do not relate to capacity or even attitudes and willingness to perform duties, they should receive sympathetic treatment from the person's supervisor. If necessary, the person's duties should be rearranged or lightened to accommodate his temporary weakness in the administrative and communication structures.

A further factor, which may be only temporary, may be related to a person's immediate situation and subject to change if that person is, say, transferred to another department, is behaviour. Through his own behaviour a person may create a barrier to effective communication and be thought of or described in terms of conflict with his fellow members of staff, his subordinates or his superiors. A Zalenzik postulates a pattern of subordinancy as follows (Zalenzik 49):

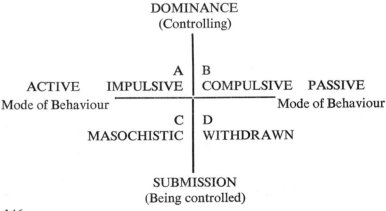

DOMINANCE
(Controlling)

	A	B	
ACTIVE	IMPULSIVE	COMPULSIVE	PASSIVE
Mode of Behaviour			Mode of Behaviour
	C	D	
	MASOCHISTIC	WITHDRAWN	

SUBMISSION
(Being controlled)

146

The four patterns of subordinancy he identifies can be described as 1 impulsive (dominant-active), 2 compulsive (dominant-passive), 3 masochistic (submissive-active) and 4 withdrawn (submissive-passive).

Two factors favour the prevalence of compulsive or masochistic patterns so far as subordinate staff are concerned in libraries, that is staff with an intelligent independent outlook or frame of mind but who nevertheless recognise the value and necessity of accepting general library goals and authority structures. Firstly, any individual member of staff experiences need for approval and recognition, which is satisfied in so far as he conforms to patterns of behaviour, attitudes and work of other staff around him. In this sense he is under pressure to conform, although usually pressure is limited to common sense or, if necessary, senior librarians' arguments rationally based on common sense and valid statements. Secondly, in joining the library, the individual accepts authority relationships; he agrees that within some limits, possibly defined by an employment contract or job description, he will accept as the premises of his behaviour orders and instructions given him within the library. This acceptance gives the library administrators a strong means of influencing the individual and is itself enhanced by the professionalisation of library jobs (other than non-professional or manual jobs). The professional librarian has undergone a formal training, usually shares a common background with his fellow workers and is inclined to accept formal regulation and supervision of his duties.

Acceptance by staff of professional ideals and standards, levels of library service and authority structures, will not eliminate all conflict of behaviour. Some measure of ambiguity is inevitable in all organisations; to attempt the creation of a complete organisational blueprint, in which every task would be specified, every method prescribed and every contingency foreseen, would be a self-defeating effort. It would be impossibly costly, would be constantly upset by change and would be anathema to intelligent professional workers (Saltonstall 387). Where the source of staff conflict is genuine uncertainty, organisational arrangements should be available for settling such disputes. Where conflict results from a clash of personalities, organisational arrangements should similarly provide a solution and perhaps dictate a change of functions or move of personnel to another department; in a new or different situation personal reactions and conflict could well be reduced or minimised. Where conflict results from ambiguity of situation or ambiguity of action or responsibility in face of a unique situation, such conflict cannot be eliminated but the attempt should be made to contain these conditions at all levels and in forms compatible with individual dignity and importance and overall library interest. The attempt is most likely to be successful, of course, if senior administrative staff are themselves well trained and experienced in the field of personnel management and are sympathetically seeking a compatibility between sound organisational structure and channels of communication, and individual enthusiasm and feelings.

The above discussion relates mainly to the individual, his personality traits and attitudes. A great deal of behaviour which has been supposed to emanate from within the individual, to be based on his fixed character traits, is in fact a function of the individual within his group. Thus, for example, an individual's position and intelligence determines whether he perceives a discrepancy between his responsibility and control; the manner in which he chooses to respond to it may well be affected by the opinions and responses of his immediate colleagues. Behaviour is the product of two things: the nature of the individual that behaves and the nature of the situation in which the individual finds himself. The situation is a source of stimulation; behaviour is always the individual's response to a stimulation from his environment. The situation, however, can be significantly different for an individual on his own and the individual who forms part of a working group. In the latter case group feeling and interpretation will condition the way in which the situation is viewed. Hence group affiliations are of great significance for library administrative structure and communication systems.

Group affiliations and attitudes are often discussed in relation to morale, which may be defined as the attitudes of individuals and groups toward their work environment and toward voluntary cooperation to the full extent of their ability in the best interests of the organisation (Davis, 1957 444). Group morale is more important than individual morale (unless all or many staff, as individuals, are affected by adverse morale), since it can have a greater effect upon staff cohesion and communication.

One difficulty involved in discussing behaviour and morale is that it is hard to distinguish a motivation or existence of good morale from a description of behaviour. There is no guarantee that a particular act or mode of behaviour, which the observer takes to spring from a particular motivation or degree of morale, does in fact have that motivation or morale as its prime driving force, its prime causation. If behaviour, individual actions, contribute to library services in accordance with library goals and appear to give satisfaction to the individual worker, then the most that can be claimed is that it is assumed that such actions may spring from certain motivation and sense of morale and in turn contribute to library morale.

There is, similarly, no way of measuring how much of a need or motivation is fulfilled by an action; nor is it possible to describe what a person's state is at any time in terms of these needs (Starr 602). Again, it is possible only to generalise about possible degrees of satisfaction. A library can, however, at least consciously construct its personnel facilities and work at staff relations in an effort to satisfy some of these needs.

A number of behavioural scientists have postulated theories concerning the factors that motivate people and lead to satisfaction and morale. Abraham Maslow developed the concept that the needs of human beings are organised in a series of levels, ranging from the root physiological needs (such as hunger) at the base to self-actualisation (the need to realise one's own potential) at the apex (Maslow Cht 6).

In 1957 Douglas McGregor published his now famous theory— the theory X and theory Y (McGregor, 1960). He pointed out that there are two contrasting points of view about how to manage an organisation, such views being based on concepts of human behaviour and motivation. He saw the usual point of view embodying ideas such as:

1 most human beings dislike work and will avoid it if they can

2 they have little or no ambition, dislike responsibility and prefer to be led

3 they are self-centred and are indifferent to the needs of the organisation

4 they resist change and above all want security

5 they are not very bright and they are easily misled by demagogues.

This whole set of beliefs and assumptions, and the style of management based on them, McGregor called theory X. Such a theory does not, however, provide for the effective motivation of people whose physical and safety needs are satisfied and whose social and egotistic needs are therefore dominant. To provide a better understanding of human nature than is to be found in the theory X assumptions, he put forward theory Y. The latter consists of a series of ideas or assumptions that have been supported by the findings of other social scientists. These assumptions are:

1 Human beings do not necessarily dislike work. They may enjoy it or they may not. If the work is a source of satisfaction to them, they will perform it willingly. If not or if it is a source of punishment, then, of course, they will avoid it.

2 Direction, control, reward and the threat of punishment are not the only means to get people to work for organisational goals. Human beings will work hard and well to achieve objectives they believe in.

3 The satisfaction of egotistic needs (for achievement, recognition, self-confidence, etc) can come about as people work toward these objectives that they have adopted.

4 Under the right conditions, the average human being wants and will seek responsibility.

5 Imagination, ingenuity and creativity are characteristics most human beings, not just a few, possess. By and large, people do not get the opportunity to display such characteristics in modern industry. When they do, the industry benefits.

The key task of administrative staff is to arrange things so that they and other staff can work together for the success of the enterprise. McGregor termed this the principle of integration and it is similar to the participative system detailed by Rensis Likert in *New patterns in management.*

Assuming the satisfaction of basic physiological needs relating to lighting and heating, this system involves creating, at every level of staff, a feeling of real responsibility for the organisation's services and goals and maximum output of effort to attain them. It also involves real participation in decision making through consultation and communication, the free expression of ideas and mutual trust. Participation is more than getting consent for something already decided. It is a social and psychological relationship among people, which is stimulated by continuous association and discussion amongst these people.

The relevance of McGregor's Y theory, as opposed to his X

theory, to librarians will be appreciated in the light of statements made above concerning adhesion and common interests of professional employees. Personal purposes and processes learned prior to employment in a library, as well as experience outside the particular library whilst a member of the library profession, mean that a certain amount of information extraneous to, or even in conflict with, library purpose and action will always be present in the human sector or organisational structure. But too much repression or subordination of personal goals to organisational needs may result in lowered efficiency, so that a library's aim should be to find a balance between organisational and individual needs and personalities which will result in library efficiency and individual satisfaction.

Junior and non-professional staff are primarily motivated by job content. Thus, whereas a more senior professional member of staff may be prepared to work at a boring task, for a time at least, finding comfort in the fact that it is contributing to library services in a valuable way and that its accomplishment may lead to more interesting and rewarding tasks, the attention of the junior or non-professional member of staff will be more closely linked to a view of his immediate tasks. Yet there are common factors which encourage a sense of satisfaction and appreciation of library goals, factors common to all library staff. As well as the work itself, which should be reasonably interesting to a person of a particular level of intelligence thought suitable for the job performance, other factors include sense of achievement; expressed recognition (of work done) by supervisory staff; delegated responsibility commensurate with particular tasks; the possibility of advancement, if not within the library profession or the individual library, at least possible advance to other work tasks in the same library job and department.

The existence of these factors will not necessarily guarantee morale or increased effort, since the relationship between staff attitudes and work output or efficiency is not clear-cut. The encouragement of these factors, however, is a task of all librarians in administrative or supervisory positions and is the basis of sound mangement. The existence and encouragement of these factors usually takes place within the group, that is in the context of the working group in a particular department, and is facilitated or hindered by group reactions and feelings. Group feelings are

151

particularly important in so far as the junior or non-professional worker is concerned, that is workers who may lack general library or professional motivations. Hindrances may arise because the group is not given clear lines of responsibility in relation to library activities and hence group administrative arrangements may mitigate against individual satisfaction.

The factors themselves help to stimulate individual satisfaction as well as group loyalty and thus provide an excellent basis for communication with all staff. However, it is not easy to separate communication from the other listed factors in such an easy manner. Good communication will facilitate the establishment and promotion of factors such as recognition and will in turn be aided by the existence of these factors. Hence, as has been emphasised a number of times, communication is closely bound up with organisational structure and good communication is closely related to sound administration.

An Australian personnel expert, P H Cook, has suggested that the efforts to improve morale through improved communication are entirely misdirected. According to him, morale does not depend on communication; instead communication depends on morale. In other words there has to be an atmosphere favouring rather than interfering with successful communication (Cook). In support of Cook's statements T M Higham, an English psychologist, asserted that ' the pathetic notion that you can improve communications by giving more and better information should surely be allowed to die a natural death; you will not get any reception if you are not trusted, but if relations are good, then there is a good chance that what you say will be received, and that you will get co-operation in return ' (Higham 4-5).

These statements certainly support the implication of this chapter, that morale is an aid to communication, but one may take a less dogmatic view of the precise relationship between morale and communication. Certainly a level of morale or receptive attitudes is a necessary prerequisite of successful communication but, as stated above, communication in turn can facilitate staff satisfaction and morale by keeping staff supplied with information and comments about library activities and their own work and levels of achievement. The latter situation is particularly likely to occur if such communication is perceived by staff to be useful and genuine.

152

Dispersal and isolation

Communications in an organisation, say an office or a library, will be of three main types:

1 personal, involving the movement of people, whether for the purpose of direct discussion or to carry papers and materials from one place to another

2 papers and related materials. These may be moved by hand or by mechanical equipment

3 audio visual. Communication by telephone, intercom or closed circuit television.

The first category is clearly the most important so far as physical distance or distribution of staff is concerned. Walking unrealistic distances can involve considerable waste of staff time. The movement of papers usually only involves an undue wastage of time if the movement is other than a normal routine or really exaggerated physical distances are involved. Audio visual communication does not rely on physical proximity for its effectiveness and has little effect on the relative locations of users.

The majority of office blocks, save for recent ' open plan ' or ' landscaped ' offices, have narrow plans with rooms on either side of a corridor and, although pedestrian communication is to this extent predetermined, it is extended in comparison with that existing in a building which groups staff in larger departments. In the planning of libraries, in aligning the three elements of users, material and staff within certain spatial relationships, the relation of material and staff to users (communication between stock and user) has usually led to an emphasis on large reading room structures to facilitate contact between stock and user with the staff performing useful intermediary functions. Even in the largest and most modern library building, the contrast with office blocks is still evident. The library may resemble an office block so far as physical structure is concerned (*eg* part of Queen's University Library, Belfast), yet numerous corridors and small rooms give way, in library buildings, to larger rooms (reading rooms or subject departments, plus functional departments such as cataloguing) with a greater concentration of staff groupings. Only in the case of the librarian and other senior administrative staff is there the likelihood of separation or isolation in small offices. If the necessitated movement of other senior staff around a large building sometimes makes contact, as opposed to general staff communication, difficult, this can be solved by such

153

persons carrying 'bleepers'. The system is mainly in evidence in hospitals but is used with advantage in Edinburgh University Library.

The effect of such physical arrangement in libraries is that in medium-sized and large systems isolation of administrative staff can lead to excessive use of the telephone and memos for communicating with other parts of the library. So far as the rest of the staff are concerned, however, their everyday movements and hence to a good extent their communications, move along similar traffic patterns to the library users, when working with readers and relating their needs and demands to the material available in the collection (Bassnett 105).

Any studies of staff working relationships made whilst planning a new library or physical rearrangement of a reading room or functional department (eg cataloguing) are made primarily from the point of the flow of materials and user access. This is not a criticism of library planners, nor an indication that they usually ignore staff communication when working out their ideas. Library staff communication is important in so far as it adds to the efficiency of the user–stock relationship. If this relationship is improved by good planning, then it follows that lines of staff communication, as a functional contribution to library service, will probably be improved also. Whether these lines of communication are wisely or adequately used is another consideration. Also, a further factor to be taken into account is that communication lines are additionally determined by administrative arrangements of staff structure, which may vary in a given physical building. Yet the fact remains that if sensible attention is paid to user–stock relationships this will obviously affect staff alignment and grouping and should facilitate staff communication in a work context.

The above discussion relates largely to individual buildings, say, central libraries. One probelm facing many libraries of all types is a scattering of staff and stock over what often amounts to considerable geographic distances with the provision of branch or departmental libraries. An important qualifying factor in a discussion of the disadvantages for staff communication of geographic distance is that physical distance or proximity is affected and conditioned by mental attitudes. Good communication and understanding is itself related to personal links and familiarity between persons, hence such links and familiarity can often break down or overcome geographic barriers.

154

In a library system subject to geographic dispersal the employment of such techniques or practices as regular rotation of staff, visits of senior staff to outlying sections and visits of all categories of staff to the central library, can aid communication and understanding between staff.

Dispersed collections usually result from considerations of convenience and service. It may be more convenient for the public to use a county branch library in a small town than travel forty miles to the county hq library; in a university library, arguments concerning desirability of having close working access to materials has often resulted in separate department or faculty libraries for medicine, law and music. This development may take place over a number of years and be somewhat haphazard rather than planned, as in the early history of the University of California Library at Berkeley (Peterson 39-43), or may be deliberately planned, as in the Library of University College, Cardiff. Such deliberation may, however, be phased over a number of years. A more immediate diffusion of a library may, paradoxically, result from sudden amalgamation. This situation has arisen in relation to government libraries (*eg* Mintech), as a result of ministerial changes and academic libraries as a result of an amalgamation of various educational units to form a higher status institution. Thus the library of the Polytechnic of Central London has seven separate divisions scattered around its fourteen buildings, involving a total walking distance of several miles (Ashworth 274).

It can be said that extreme geographic distance presents no great communication problem; the distance is accepted, sections of the library are organised and run as virtually separate units and hence no frustrating attempt is made to maintain the level of communication links which would be thought necessary or desirable in a small system. Several American universities have off-campus units; these are institutions which are under the sponsorship of, and bear the name of, a large college or university located elsewhere. Distances involved may be several hundred miles. Thus at the University of Nevada, the Southern Regional Division at Las Vegas is located 500 miles from the main campus at Rene; 165 miles separate the Duluth campus of the University of Minnesota and its parent institution. In such systems the administrative arrangements are such that the larger off-campus libraries are autonomous and, although some of their libraries might in theory be in ambiguous positions between the head librarian on the main campus and the off-campus administration, the administrative lines are usually clearly defined (Ryan 542-3).

Where distances are not as great as in these examples, bad communication and misunderstanding may lead to the assumption of virtual autonomy by departmental libraries. Such autonomy will not lead to satisfactory library service or staff relationships, however, since it is not a recognised or planned feature of the whole library administrative structure. Rather is it a sign of administrative weaknesses and misunderstandings. In 1960 a report revealed the existence of such a situation in Rutgers University Library. Here geographic distances are not particularly great. The university library includes the libraries of the university facilities in Newark and Camden, plus those in some five widely separated campuses in New Brunswick. Distances involved, however, are not as great as in the case of the University of Nevada. New Brunswick is twenty miles south west of Newark, with Camden a further fifty miles south west of New Brunswick.

Bad staff and administrative relations, however, tended to exaggerate the geographic distances involved. Extracts from the report read as follows:

' Many staff members seem to lack any clear understanding of the relationship of the libraries one to another, of the functions of the central library, and the duties of departmental heads and librarians of comparable rank. There is uncertainty about lines of administrative authority, and there is widespread lack of knowledge of the overall policies of the library. Where policies are known there is sometimes an inability to interpret them easily. Written procedures are unavailable in some libraries and departments, and existing procedures are infrequently examined and modified ' (MacDonald 108-9).

' . . . the library would benefit from closer supervision and greater effort to codify its activities. This need is especially strong within the central library. There are striking contrasts apparent in the attitudes of many branch librarians. On the one hand there is resentment of centralized administrative control and on the other there is the desire for a closer relationship among the libraries of the system. A sense of isolation or remoteness is common, as are complaints about a lack of information concerning professional affairs in general and central library affairs in particular. There is

156

interest in having a greater voice in the formation of university library policy. An insufficient acquaintance among staff members of the various libraries is a frequently mentioned problem. In short, there is a great need to foster among the staff the feeling of belonging to a common enterprise. Other problems for branch librarians have to do with unclear lines of administrative authority, their division of loyalty between the various deans and the librarian of the university, and service difficulties involving several departments of the central library ' (Ibid 111).

To overcome these difficulties the report recommended the establishment of a staff association; the establishment of a regular procedure for discussing the problems and needs of the branch libraries and improving the means of formulating and enunciating library policy in a democratic manner; regularly scheduled meetings of all head librarians and the librarian of the university; exchanges of library personnel in order to enlarge the experience of the staff and promote a feeling of communicating among the libraries; the establishment of a reasonable degree of uniformity in procedures and services in all parts of the library system. Such provisions are virtually commonsense in running any large or dispersed organisation but it is interesting and useful to find an example of a library where their absence resulted in poor staff relationships, with obvious effects on library service and book provision.

Even a small, relatively compact, system may be subject to geographic dispersal. Thus Bath University Library, with a staff of 25 (March 1972), has two branch libraries: the Northgate branch, which is one mile from the central library and the Rockwell branch, which is 20 miles from central. Admittedly the branches are small, each staffed full-time by one person, with regular visits of staff to and from central but dispersal is still present.

Although British university libraries are not subject to the geographic dispersal evident in many American universities, problems of dispersal, albeit over comparatively small geographic distances, do exist. Liverpool University Library, for example, has 20 service points and finds it a difficult problem achieving satisfactory communication in such a decentralised structure. Where departmental library divisions are fewer and perhaps more marked, responsibility for day-to-day administration and departmental communication seems to be delegated to librarians in charge of the departmental libraries. Birmingham University Library, for example, includes three faculty libraries, each supervised by a sub-librarian. These libraries are the Barnes Medical Library with a stock of 55,000 volumes, 1,000 periodicals and a staff of 11; the Harding Law Library with 17,000 volumes, 90 periodicals and a staff of 2; and the Music Library with a stock of 4,000 volumes, 30,000 orchestral and vocal scores and parts, 20,000 pieces of sheet music, 6,000 gramophone records and a staff of 2. Although these libraries are only five minutes walk from the central library, it is found administratively convenient to leave sub-librarians to organise the day-to-day running of their libraries. New staff are taken on a visit to the libraries but there are no regular visits to or from the main library.

Delegation of responsibility for communication and day-to-day administrative supervision within a section of the library seems to be more justified in county systems, where geographic area covered may be 70 by 50 miles as in Somerset or 80 by 40 miles as in Lancashire. In Hertfordshire each of the three divisions (West, East and Mid Herts) is under the control of a divisional librarian and his deputy, who exercise their control in such fields as staffing and book selection. Most day-to-day library work and hence communication in Hertfordshire does, in fact, revolve around the division. In the field of staffing, junior appointments are made at the divisional level. Senior staff induction is dealt with at divisional level, the form and formality depending upon the divisional librarian and his deputy, often in consultation with the library's county training officer. Apart from trainees, as a general rule, staff are appointed to a particular post and remain in that position until they successfully apply for another. So far as book selection is concerned, with the exception of special stocks such as music, playsets, local history material and books for adult classes, all adult book selection takes place initially within the three divisions.

Links between the various units of Hertfordshire's system are in part fostered by a programme of visits. The county librarian makes occasional systematic tours of all service points as well as specific extra visits as need arises. The deputy county librarian visits all service points at least twice a year and aims at more frequent calls. Extra visits are also necessary for specific purposes. All departmental heads at hq (music librarian, local history librarian, etc) visit service points from time to time, while the county bibliographical officer and the county cataloguer meet regularly with the divisional bibliographical officers. Within the divisions, divisional librarians and their deputies maintain ad hoc but fairly frequent contacts with the various service points and staff.

Many county libraries have regular visits to and from central hq to regions and branches, the pattern being quite varied. Few such libraries, however, arrange visits for junior or part-time staff. Exceptions include Staffordshire County where, apart from visiting hq on the induction course (arranged annually—one day a week for 13 weeks), junior staff may be brought to hq on the branch librarian's monthly visit, when he will show the junior the departments at hq. In Flintshire County Library all members of the full-time staff visit hq at least once a week, on one complete day, on a rota system, to become fully acquainted with all routines such as computer cataloguing; part-time branch staff visit hq for quarterly meetings and also as often as required for book stock supplementation and so on.

Such a pattern of visiting, supplemented where possible by rotation of staff, helps hq and branch staff to get to know each other and facilitates understanding and communication. Yet, of course, the amount of visiting and rotation of staff required to produce satisfactory levels of staff communication and library service will vary from one library system to another, depending on factors such as the number of staff employed. In widely dispersed systems, such as Cumberland and Lancashire, it is possible to waste a great deal of time attempting to promote too many staff visits; such visits could have a disruptive effect on timetable arrangements and staffing of service points and could be detrimental to library service. Some form of balance must be sought by the librarian, based on a knowledge of his local resources and circumstances.

Municipal systems in Britain are not subject to such degrees of geographic dispersal as counties, although distances involved may be quite substantial so far as city travel is concerned. Thus the City of Coventry is approximately ten miles in diameter, that of Birmingham sixteen miles. The pattern of visits varies as it does in county libraries. Regular visits are usually undertaken by limited numbers and categories of staff, staff in one branch or area or the whole system possibly meeting occasionally as groups. General staff meetings are obviously difficult to arrange even in a medium-sized system like Luton Public Library, intruding as they do upon library opening hours and degrees of service.

In large systems it may prove impossible to organise meetings for all staff. Thus in Camden Libraries staff meetings tend to be limited to subject or service groups (*eg* monthly meetings of branch librarians with the director at hq). General staff meetings on a more localised basis have been started in Holborn, for the staff of this library, and are being considered by St Pancras and Hampstead libraries. One disadvantage resulting from such a development is that branch staff may feel, in fact be, left somewhat out in the cold. Writing in the Camden Libraries' staff news letter one assistant branch librarian expressed the view:

' There is no doubt that we in the branches are not au fait with all that is going dynamically on at the central library—despite the *Newsletter*. This is due to all sorts of reasons; the fact that the branch delivery system is not perfect; that perhaps it's your day off when something important happens; but above all that we don't have the opportunity to exchange interesting items of professional interest with members of other departments over coffee. It is in this informal contact that ideas breed best; and alas I can think of no way to cope with this problem ' (*News for Camden Libraries and Arts Staff,* Dec 1971 11).

This assistant, perhaps a naturally gregarious person, concludes with a reflection on informal communication. Lack of everyday immediate contact with other groups of staff in other branches or at central is just not possible in a decentralised system; it is one of the inherent factors in, or consequences of, such an arrangement. Much the same may be said for formal communication; immediate face-to-face contact is reduced to occasions of visits and a certain sense of detachment, even isolation, is bound to affect some staff. Certain members of staff may welcome such isolation of their immediate working group, say a branch library staff, from undue outside interference as they might interpret hq control. In the study of Rutgers University Library referred to above the investigator found that although a sense of isolation was common among branch librarians, some displayed a resentment of centralised administrative control. This could have been resentment against inefficiency, against uncoordinated elements of bureaucratic control but it is still fair to say that in most libraries some individual members of staff will favour comparative isolation and value what they feel to be a sense of independence.

For most members of staff, however, undue isolation can lead to inefficiency, misinterpretation of the library policy affecting service or idiosyncratic modifications and a sense of frustration. Whatever degree of independence is granted to individuals in the performance of their duties, whatever degree of isolation is welcomed by some members of staff, certain levels of contact throughout the system are necessary to secure degrees of efficiency in service and cooperation among staff.

The comments by the assistant branch librarian in Camden's news letter provoked an editorial reply in the next issue. The editor indicated that branch librarians can do a lot to combat a sense of isolation among their staff by their personal enthusiasm and willingness to communicate news concerning library developments elsewhere. Where this enthusiasm was evident the branches ' hummed with activity and participation ' and staff ' felt very much a part of Camden Libraries ' (Ibid, Jan 1972 1).

The editor went on to comment that ' insularity is a frame of mind '. This reinforces something said at the beginning of this discussion of geographic dispersal, namely that reaction to distance is in part conditioned by mental attitudes. Obviously a mental attitude that dismisses geographic distances as being inconsequential may not result in the overriding of all disadvantages accruing from dispersal but it should help to dispel individual unease.

Similar comments can be made looking at communication and geographic dispersal from the point of view of the librarian and administrators, as opposed to the outlying staff. Here again, a mental attitude, in the form of an awareness of the difficulties is a help, although admittedly no form of complete solution. The whole problem of effective staff management and communication in a diffused system is not an easy one to solve. Each system will have its own unique circumstances and difficulties but, in all systems, certain administrative arrangements can help to overcome the common and the unique difficulties. Such arrangements are:

1 Clear lines of delegated responsibility in administration and communication should be established for staff responsible for particular departments or units, *eg* regional librarians. If possible, duties and responsibilities should be in writing. This will facilitate cooperation by removing uncertainties relating to duties and lines of communication.

2 Regularly scheduled visits. The number of these will depend on local conditions and resources but they should encompass a

161

two way traffic from hq to branches and vice versa and if possible involve junior and part-time staff as well as seniors. However few these visits, if they are planned and scheduled regularly, staff awareness of this fact may well help to overcome frustration resulting from a combination of isolation and uncertainty as to links with hq.

3 General staff meetings. Most dispersed systems will find it impossible to arrange meetings for all staff, although it might be worthwhile experimenting with an annual meeting. Otherwise the grouping should be as large as possible, say, within a region or branch and should be scheduled to occur at least four times a year.

4 Rotation of staff. If travelling arrangements make this practicable, it should be considered for junior and senior staff; in the former case after periods of between six and twelve months in one particular post, in the latter case after periods of between one and two years.

5 Written communication. The above personal contacts should be supplemented by adequate written communication in the form of a monthly staff news sheet and memos on any important developments affecting the whole system (*eg* local government reorganisation). Copies of these should be sent to all staff. They will perhaps be distributed by regional or branch librarians, who should also have the responsibility for distributing written communications relating to more localised sections of the library or even individual members of staff.

6 Informal communication. A dispersed university or municipal system will find it easier to arrange staff guild meetings than a county system. Such meetings, however, do have value in helping staff to become acquainted with other workers in the system and might be supplemented by a staff guild magazine.

The above arrangements will not necessarily produce the perfect library system or solve all communication difficulties. Physical distance reduces the opportunities for checking on the performance of subordinates and it is often the actual frequency of such supervisory visits or review, rather than the official definition of the levels of responsibility, that governs the amount of discretion subordinates can and must exercise. Yet if the implementation of the above arrangements is accompanied by a sympathetic awareness of difficulties, at least the worst aspects of dispersal, such as feelings of isolation and uncoordinated library services, may be remedied.

Looking specifically at communication, as opposed to staff and administrative arrangements and structures, in the light of the above statements, it can be said that the librarian must aim for some sort of balance between volume of communication and degree of dispersal difficulties. There is no easy answer to the question ' How much communication?', just as there is no easy solution to the problem of geographic dispersal or decentralisation. Answers to these questions and problems must be sought through the exercise of the managerial skills of senior librarians, utilising theoretical and practical experience in dealing with local conditions existing in their particular library. Staff communication is essentially an adaptive process applied to particular circumstances by persons with particular abilities and insights into staff management.

CHAPTER EIGHT

A communication programme

IN AN organisation, decisions may be made on an ad hoc basis and problems handled as they arise. One disadvantage of such a style of management is that action may not be related to organisational purposes and attention may be focused merely on the results of particular occurrences. Such a disadvantage can be eliminated if administrative staff look ahead and take action according to guidelines established in connection with plans relating to, say, communication.

A form of communication programme, such as that detailed in this chapter, could with advantage be adopted by any library, whatever its size and however good or bad the existing communication position is in the eyes of the administrative staff. A programme leads to an examination of library and personal effectiveness and has advantages over and above any possible plan implementation. A communication programme should be seen as a general contribution to the administrative process of ensuring ability to meet service requirements and making the most effective use of all available resources. A programme encompasses tasks of management, as opposed to activities of operating (*eg* sending out orders for books) and is a proper subject for study by library administrators.

The terms 'programme' and 'plan' are closely linked. The Association of Research Libraries defines planning, in its broadest sense, as ' an orderly means used by an organisation to establish effective control of its own future. The administrative group is engaged in planning when it selects and defines the organisation's philosophy and objectives and determines the means required to achieve them ' (ARL 20). A more limited view may be taken of ' planning ' or ' plan '. Plans are a statement, prepared in advance, of what is to be done. They are based on objectives and form the means by which it is proposed to convert the present condition to some future condition. Closely linked to this concept of plan are preliminary tasks of objective definition and investigation of the existing situation, and subsequent tasks of plan implementation and modification. To this overall combination of tasks or elements may be assigned the description ' programme '; its elements can be presented in diagrammatic form thus:

Establishment→Investigation→Plan→Schedule→Implementation→Revision
      of   of existing
  objectives   situation

A schedule is a plan plus timings, that is a plan geared to action. Implementation of the plan is closely linked to control and the mechanism for ensuring that people carry out plans is in turn linked to the notions of plan revision and evaluation. The latter are continuous processes undertaken during and after the period of initial plan implementation.

Objectives

A communication programme could include the following foci of attention and express certain general aims:

Foci	*Aims*
Whole library	Improve communication links and effectiveness as a contribution to improved levels of library service and staff morale.
Individual departments	Encouragement of good inter- and intra-departmental communication to facilitate the internal workings of the library.
Individual persons	Ensure certain levels of communication proficiency as a requirement for adequate performance of tasks associated with the individual's job.
	Ensure adequate understanding by the individual of his role in the department and library—what he is responsible for and how he personally is a part of the whole system.
	Carefully distinguish areas of responsibility to eliminate unnecessary overlaps and duplication of effort.

165

6*

The identifiable elements of an objective are 1 time, 2 quantity, 3 quality and 4 cost. Time structures specify within what period it is desired to accomplish certain things. Here a compromise must be sought between long-term and short-term criteria. An objective set for too short a period may turn out to be nothing more than a prediction; at the moment of objective formation it could well have appeared obvious that the objective would in fact be achieved. A long term objective, on the other hand, may simply be the expression of a hope or vague wish, which may not materialise in practice since the period of time encompasses too many uncontrollable events. Objectives are most effectively geared to quarterly, six monthly or yearly periods and the yearly period is the one chosen for the programme forming the contents of this chapter.

Quantity is perhaps the most easily identifiable of the four elements. It relates to questions of how many or how much (*eg* how many written directives to issue in a certain time relating to a certain matter). The question of cost will be dealt with in a later section of this chapter. Quality is a more subjective factor and the least satisfactory so far as the practical establishment of objectives or a plan is concerned. It is difficult, for example, to formulate guidelines for the implementation of a plan whose objectives are expressed in such general terms as ' improve staff morale '. Hence the aims listed above against foci of attention need to be redefined in a quantifiable sense before a workable plan can be drawn up.

Objectives obviously relate not only to the library as an organisation but also to its individual staff members. Hence any listing of objectives must be associated with staff positions, abilities and tasks. Such a consideration approaches the definition of management by objectives provided by Reddin as ' a method of associating objectives with positions and linking these objectives together with the corporate plan ' (Reddin 16). Restating the problem, objectives must be geared to the administrative structure of the library, to the personnel it possesses, their areas of responsibility and abilities, and to library activities.

Assignment of communication responsibilities must be based on of staff communication and related areas of administration as bility, otherwise functions and responsibilities may tend to diverge. A librarian, for example, might see his responsibilities in the field of staff communication and related areas of administration as covering:

Staff recruitment
Staff training
Coordination
Organisation of staff meetings
Overall responsibility for staff communication
Staff counselling

In fact, if properly analysed, the librarian's unique contribution may well be limited to a more restricted field of activities. The true structure of responsibility might be:

Librarian: personnel policy
Deputy librarian: administrative effectiveness

Other areas of activity are primarily the responsibility of other senior members of staff as follows:

Staff recruitment: deputy librarian
Staff training: deputy librarian plus departmental heads
Organisation of staff meetings: chief assistant
Responsibility for written communications: most senior staff
Staff counselling: departmental heads and chief assistant (only rarely the librarian)

Hence an objective, dealing with, say, staff training would need to be related to the positions and abilities of deputy and departmental heads, rather than the librarian.

Staff abilities are an important consideration since obviously certain levels of skill are necessary for the performance of tasks such as writing a memo or conducting a staff training session. Hence, when formulating objectives in a library, one must assess what important communication skills are required in each position (*eg* heads of departments) and what levels or standards of proficiency are needed in tasks and operations relating to these positions. With such considerations relating to the library's staff positions, tasks and abilities in mind it is now possible to present a list of objectives in quantifiable terms:

General aims	*Quantifiable objectives*
Whole library	
Improve communication links and effectiveness as a contribution to improved levels of library service and staff morale.	Issue a written statement of library communication policy, including an indication of library goals. Establish annual staff meetings for all staff and monthly meetings for a) senior, b)

junior staff. Examine the functions and content of the staff news sheet with an aim of improving its effectiveness. Institute a series of irregular administrative memos on important topics (*eg* local government reorganisation).

Individual departments

Encourage good inter- and intra-departmental communication to facilitate the internal workings of the library and the efficiency of departmental heads.

Establish monthly meetings for heads of departments.

Encourage the establishment of individual departmental meetings according to need as seen by departmental heads. Examine function and content of existing inter-departmental communications.

Institute training sessions for departmental heads in staff communication. Seek to ensure personal (*ie* dept head) efficiency by six monthly appraisal interviews.

Individual persons

Ensure certain levels of communication proficiency as a requirement for adequate performance of tasks associated with the individual's job.

Improve understanding by the individual of his role in the department and library—his specific responsibilities and how he personally is a part of the whole system.

Departmental heads to prepare job specifications for individual staff members. To be supplemented by departmental staff manuals.

Then determine what communication skills and levels of proficiency are required for particular jobs; examine current levels of effectiveness and introduce individual and group training.

Establish induction training for new senior staff (one week) and juniors (3 days). Ensure adequate representation of all departments in a) working groups, b) staff news sheet items.

The listing of objectives will, of course, vary from library to library. In all cases the listing could be linked to time schedules, although it is usually more appropriate to add definite timings to a plan rather than a list of objectives, which may well be in draft form prior to the enumeration of the existing communication situation. This examination helps to determine how adequate the system is to its tasks and to finalise the listing of quantifiable objectives as part of a comprehensive plan.

Examination of the existing situation

The examination of the existing communication situation (*ie* a combination of policy and practice) will be closely linked to the formulation of a communication plan. Even if no desire is felt to introduce a detailed communication plan after surveying the existing situation, the latter task must still be undertaken with certain objectives of a communication system, and certain ideals, in mind. Obviously, objectives and ideals figure prominently in any communication plan, hence the link between plan and investigation. This link can further be seen if a method of investigation is adopted as follows:

1 identify the problems to be faced and the ends to be accomplished

2 gather data relevant to the problem and ends

3 analyse the data

4 formulate a plan (possibly including certain alternative elements. *eg* the case could be argued for a) a formal staff news sheet or b) a staff magazine incorporating features of a formal news sheet plus those of a staff guild magazine geared to the library concerned)

5 determine whether to a) introduce this plan, b) parts of it only or c) leave the communications situation as it was before the investigation.

As will be appreciated, even an investigation of the existing communication situation in a library may require extensive time and intensive effort. The formulation of a plan, which will more clearly establish differences between existing and required standards, will involve even more time and effort. Perhaps the extreme alternative methods of investigation can be indicated by quoting from two sources. On the one hand, an Industrial Society publication recommends giving a young person, such as a professional trainee, the job of examining communication (Garnett 25). On the other hand,

J H Ottemiller outlines the case for employing a management consultant to investigate a particular administrative area or problem (Ottemiller).

The former method would be a valuable exercise for the trainee concerned and would undoubtedly bring to light opinions and situations which might remain latent or unexpressed during a more formal investigation. The major disadvantage would probably be that the trainee would lack sufficient experience and administrative knowledge to frame his enquiry so as to get all of the most pertinent information. A management survey will be more closely linked to a plan in the sense that it would logically involve the submission of recommendations which form a plan for action. An outside consultant would be employed where it was felt that library staff did not have the ability or sufficient time to conduct a competent and objective investigation or where a fresh outside opinion was required, especially if library staff were not familiar with all aspects of communication policies and practices. The main disadvantages of employing outside professional assistance relate to cost and time of library staff involved in facilitating the investigation and acquainting the investigator with background situations. To the latter disadvantage could be added that of library staff resentment or resistance to an outside investigation.

Most libraries will probably adopt a solution or method of investigation somewhere between the two outlined above. Either the library personnel officer will conduct the investigation or a working group be established with representatives from all levels of staff.

Just as the investigator(s) may vary, so too can the means of investigation differ. They can range from a staff attitude survey, incorporating a staff questionnaire as its main feature, to a more intensive survey incorporating a number of techniques. The more intensive method could involve staff interviews, questionnaires and the delineation of channels of communication. The latter could involve the identification of two or three recent decisions which affected staff (*eg* time-table reorganisation), followed by the establishment of the reasons behind the decisions, how they were formulated (*eg* in consultation with staff) and in what manner and to what degree of effectiveness the decisions and reasons behind them were communicated to which members of staff. Such a study would reveal whether all necessary staff had been consulted and adequately informed and in what manner the decisions came to the attention

170

of other people not directly concerned with their original subject content.

Whichever means of investigation is chosen it should aim at the collection of facts and opinions. Facts, such as the form of written communication employed by the library, are comparatively easy to obtain and could be related to a check list of items indicating the categories of communication employed in the areas of spoken, written and informal communication. Opinions may well be subjective and hence lose their value as guides to accurate analysis but they can provide an important indication of levels of achievement and efficiency as opposed to the mere existence or employment of categories of communication noted on a check list.

Numerous works exist on the methods of investigating communication, of recording facts and opinions (*eg* Rubenstein & Haberstroh; Davis, Autumn 1953). All methods of research have their strengths and weaknesses and although preference is shown here for certain methods, it should be borne in mind that the manner in which the chosen method is applied is certainly as important a consideration as choice of method according to the task at hand.

The survey of opinions would best be accomplished by a questionnaire, either self-administered or interview based. With a staff of over fifty the self-administered questionnaire will most likely be favoured. Any questionnaire can aim at revealing objective data or facts and impressions or opinions, that is the respondents' own accounts and explanations. Obviously, the aims of the questionnaire should be firmly established at the drafting stage; the consideration of what information is required or looked for will affect the wording of the questionnaire. However, the structure of the questionnaire, the methodological problem of which questions are to be asked, is a prior and possibly more crucial one than that of how to ask them.

The questionnaire under consideration will be aimed at revealing opinions rather than mere facts, such as might be obtained from asking the question 'Do you get a personal copy of the library's staff news sheet?'. The answer to this will be obvious to anyone working in the library and would appear on a factual check list. More realistic and valuable factual questions might include 'What type of communications do you receive from your head of department: a) orders and instructions relative to your work? b) information on work or matters of importance relating to other departments and the library as a whole? c) assessments as to your progress and efficiency? d) opinions relating to the work of the department and the library in general? '. These questions could be preceded or supplemented by questions asking what type of communications respondents think should be received, thus indirectly revealing whether more or less information is required under relevant headings.

It is usually advisable in a questionnaire to start off with questions which contain relatively simple, emotionally inert substance, questions which encourage response rather than delicate matters of opinion, which may create suspicion or hostility on the part of the respondent (Oppenheim 44-5). The first type of question will usually be ' closed ', involving a ' forced ' choice. The second type will fall into the category of ' open-ended ' questions, which stimulate spontaneity and thought, although admittedly they may take longer to answer or be answered according to the first thought which enters the respondent's head. The two types of questions can be linked together according to aspect of communication, as in the above example on departmental heads, or designed so that the more emotive questions seeking opinions come at the end of the questionnaire.

In the specimen staff questionnaire which follows, the open-ended type of question has generally been presented, although some of the ' closed ' questions, such as the numbering of items in order of importance, may also encourage depth of thought.

Question 1 indicates means of communication and adequacy.

Question 2 is a closely related question dealing with type of information received.

Questions 3 and 4 deal with the receipt of information and staff contacts on a general library and departmental basis. Some assessment of sufficiency may be deduced from comparing what respondents say should occur with what actually does at present.

Question 5 follows up the latter points in a wider perspective, covering job, senior staff, other departments and the library as a whole.

Questions 6 and 7 indicate with whom communication is made, and by what means. If the dividing line between seniors and juniors in a particular library is not clear or will not be obvious to all respondents, alternative divisions (*eg* non-professional/professional) may be favoured or a series of questions formulated to be answered by all staff.

The interpretation of questionnaires can, of course, be misleading as was illustrated when the questionnaire was tried on limited numbers of personnel in different libraries. For example, in response to question 2 'What type of information do you receive most regularly', an employee of a public library indicated that f) 'News of trade unions and professional organisations' was the most important category. This was not, however, because that library publicised such matters as being of the greatest importance but because published information about Nalgo (*eg Public Service*) and the Library Association (*eg* news of local branch meetings) was the only type of information, among the categories listed in the questionnaire, regularly distributed among the staff or displayed on noticeboards.

In general, however, an analysis of completed questionnaires of the type given here should indicate to the librarian:

1 the most important or effective means of communication (*eg* memos)

2 the type of information most frequently received by staff

3 the sufficiency of the existing communication and staff contacts in relation to a) the individual and his job, b) individual departments and c) the library as an organisation.

This analysis should provide a sound basis for a communication plan closely geared to the requirements of the library in which the investigation has taken place. It might, for example, be seen that, although general staff communication in the form of staff news sheets and library-wide staff meetings is reasonably adequate, communication within departments needs to be improved so as to provide staff with greater job awareness. Greater efficiency and satisfaction might follow such improved communication and awareness. The library's plan could accordingly concentrate on this aspect or range of communication.

One final point may be made on administering the questionnaire. The questionnaire itself should include preliminary notes setting out the reasons for presenting it to staff, plus instruction on its completion. Alternatively, it may be presented at staff meetings. In practice perhaps a combination of these methods would offer the best explanation and guidance to members of staff completing the questionnaire.

173

Indicate whether you are: professional/non-professional, senior/junior

Name the department or branch in which you are currently based:

1 How do you receive most information about the library and your job:	Number the items a) to g) in order of importance 1 to 7
a) By written statements (*eg* staff news sheet, letters from the librarian), given to all members of staff	
b) By other written statements such as those found in Library Committee minutes or the local press	
c) By consulting the noticeboard	
d) By word of mouth from other members of staff more senior than yourself	
e) By word of mouth from other members of staff of equal status to yourself	
f) By word of mouth from other members of staff more junior than yourself	
g) By discussion at staff meetings	

2 What type of information do you receive most regularly:	Number items a) to f) in order of frequency 1 to 6
a) News of future developments of your library and its services	
b) Information relating to your job	
c) Information relating to your times of duties (*eg* days of late evening duties), and holidays	
d) News of other members of staff	
e) News of new books and developments in librarianship	
f) News of your trade union and professional organisation(s)	

Fig 4 STAFF COMMUNICATION QUESTIONNAIRE

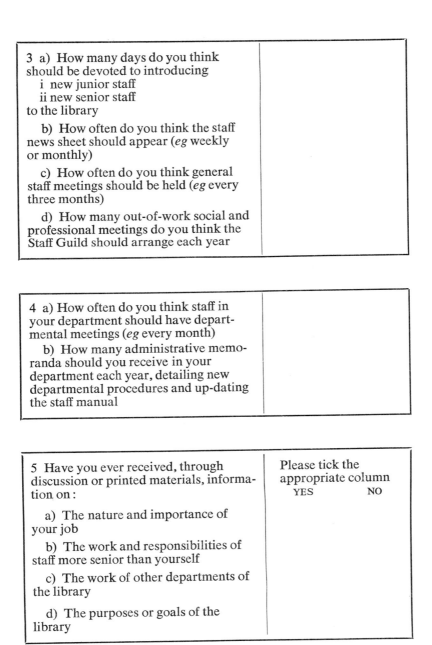

3 a) How many days do you think should be devoted to introducing i new junior staff ii new senior staff to the library b) How often do you think the staff news sheet should appear (*eg* weekly or monthly) c) How often do you think general staff meetings should be held (*eg* every three months) d) How many out-of-work social and professional meetings do you think the Staff Guild should arrange each year	

4 a) How often do you think staff in your department should have departmental meetings (*eg* every month) b) How many administrative memoranda should you receive in your department each year, detailing new departmental procedures and up-dating the staff manual	

5 Have you ever received, through discussion or printed materials, information on: a) The nature and importance of your job b) The work and responsibilities of staff more senior than yourself c) The work of other departments of the library d) The purposes or goals of the library	Please tick the appropriate column YES NO

Fig 4 STAFF COMMUNICATION QUESTIONNAIRE (*contd*)

6 (A) *To be answered by senior staff only*

Formal Communication (*ie* related to library matters, and necessary for the performance of your duties)

With whom do you have most communication (*ie* counting the sum of their communications with you and yours with them):	Number the items a) to f) in order of their importance 1 to 6	By what means are these communications made. Against items a) to f) write S (for face-to-face spoken communication) T (for telephone communication) W (for written)
a) Staff more senior than yourself in other departments (including librarian & deputy)		
b) Staff more senior than yourself in your department		
c) Other senior staff in your department		
d) Senior staff in other departments		
e) Junior staff in your department		
f) Junior staff in other departments		

Fig 4 STAFF COMMUNICATION QUESTIONNAIRE (*contd*)

6 (B) *To be answered by senior staff only*

Informal Communication (*ie* relating to library matters, such as the discussion of new members of staff, but which is not necessary for the performance of your duties; also communication on social matters)

With whom do you have most communication (*ie* counting the sum of their communications with you and yours with them):	Number items a) to f) in order of their importance 1 to 6	By what means are these communications made. Against items a) to f) write S (for face-to-face spoken communication) T (for telephone communication) W (for written)
a) Staff more senior than yourself in other departments (including librarian & deputy)		
b) Staff more senior than yourself in your department		
c) Other senior staff in your department		
d) Senior staff in other departments		
e) Junior staff in your department		
f) Junior staff in other departments		

Fig 4 STAFF COMMUNICATION QUESTIONNAIRE (*contd*)

7 (A) *To be answered by junior staff only*

Formal Communication (*ie* related to library matters, and necessary for the performance of your duties)

With whom do you have most communication (*ie* counting the sum of their communications with you and yours with them):	Number the items a) to d) in order of their importance 1 to 4	By what means are these communications made. Against items a) to d) write S (for face-to-face spoken communication) T (for telephone communication) W (for written)
a) Staff more senior than yourself in other departments (including librarian & deputy)		
b) Staff more senior than yourself in your department		
c) Other junior staff in your department		
d) Junior staff in other departments		

Fig 4 STAFF COMMUNICATION QUESTIONNAIRE (*contd*)

To be answered by junior staff only

Informal Communication (*ie* related to library matters, such as discussion of new members of staff, but which is not necessary for the performance of your duties; also communication on social matters)

With whom do you have most communication (*ie* counting the sum of their communications with you and yours with them):	Number the items a) to d) in order of their importance 1 to 4	By what means are these communications made. Against items a) to d) write S (for face-to-face spoken communication) T (for telephone communication) W (for written)
a) Staff more senior than yourself in other departments (including librarian & deputy)		
b) Staff more senior than yourself in your department		
c) Other junior staff in your department		
d) Junior staff in other departments		

Fig 4 STAFF COMMUNICATION QUESTIONNAIRE (*contd*)

Plan

A plan is a statement, prepared in advance, of what is to be, or may be, done. It links objectives (relating to the whole library, to departments and to individuals) to details revealed by an examination of the existing situation. A more complete listing of the steps involved in formulating a plan is as follows:

1 identification of the real problems to be faced and the ends to be accomplished

2 gathering facts and data relevant to the problem

3 arranging the facts

4 formulating alternative courses of action

5 choosing from among the alternatives what appears to be the best or most workable solution in the particular circumstances prevailing.

Steps 1 and 2 have been achieved in the process of formulating objectives.

It is, however, necessary to formulate the final contents of the plan by modifying the quantifiable objectives, adding what detail is thought necessary and giving thought to timings of various operations. Plans may consist of a few simple sequential steps or they may be considerably more complex. Timings can be added to the description of the plan and/or to its diagrammatic representation, in the network form.

A realistic plan which is designed with practical success in mind should exhibit the following characteristics:

1 comprehensive. It should encompass the full scope of operations

2 orderly and systematic. Steps of activity should be clear and arranged in a logical order

3 Definitive. Maximum use should be made of quantifiable data in formulating objectives and plan

4 flexible. It should respond to individual initiative and sound contributions from any member of staff

5 frequent updating. It should accommodate the need for innovations and establish progress check points

6 action and priority oriented. It must be formulated in terms of practical application and take into consideration definitions of priorities necessitated by importance of activity and limited resources (*eg* staff time).

The content of plans can obviously vary but they should encompass the three categories of objectives indicated above (*ie* whole library, departments and individuals) and should be geared to three activity levels:

1 personal changes. The designation of responsibility for communication activity as a whole (*eg* the deputy or personnel officer), or certain categories of these activities (*eg* written communication—department or service heads)

2 organisational adjustment and revision. Many features of an organisation may be employed to facilitate or control communication, *eg* location of personnel (this may include the replacement of staff or re-allocation of staff responsibilities in the light of communication achievements or failings); choice of mechanical connections between individuals and groups (such as telephones and other systems of inter-communication)

3 training programmes. Specific communication abilities are sometimes included in the list of personal characteristics required for certain jobs (*eg* teachers, salesmen) but communication skills and traits are generally not made an explicit formal part of job requirements for most positions in libraries. Difficulties arise from persons being promoted to supervisory posts without any training in supervisory skills and from lack of clarity as to exactly what levels of which abilities are needed to perform particular jobs effectively. Training programmes should cover all staff (as indeed may be said of personnel changes—item 2 above) and assist individuals to communicate more effectively and better understand the tasks and responsibilities of other members of staff. Care should be taken in formulating training programmes to emphasise such aspects of communication as acquisition and utilisation by individuals of information and so on, since communication training typically focuses on generating and disseminating information (*eg* writing skills, speech making).

If the contents of the plan accommodate the three categories of objectives and the three levels of activity, they (*ie* the contents) can be arranged on a factual basis (in the case of communication into a basic division between spoken and written communication). Each factual division will link organisational adjustment and revision to the establishment of training programmes; both will be preceded by the necessary major personnel changes. The plan will then comprise three main sections relating to:

1 personal changes

2 individual quantifiable objectives within the field of spoken communication, linked to activity steps

3 ditto—written communication.

Finally, timings can be added to the activity steps to produce a schedule. Sections of the final schedule may be written up in the form of objective record sheets (Reddin 145-54), simple forms on which are recorded programme (or schedule) areas, associated objectives, the priority of the objectives and the sequence of the activities. Additional items on the objective record sheets may relate to implementation, viz measurement method and actual performance achieved. Each objective is recorded on a separate objective record sheet, these sheets thus providing a record of objectives and a useful planning document, which can be used to formulate changes in the programme as desired. The example presented here relates to a number of combined activities in the field of written communication.

A number is assigned to each programme area. If the programme area is the fourth the librarian has established in his programme then 4 is written by the main heading. Objectives within this programme area are then numbered 1, 2, 3, etc. Such objectives are detailed on separate objective record sheets; they may be ordered in terms of priority (priority numbers thus correspond to objective numbers 1, 2, 3, etc), that is to objectives within a particular programme area or sequentially to objectives throughout the whole spectrum of programme areas in the plan, with perhaps several objectives having the same priority. Thus if an objective is the first objective for number 4 programme area, 4.1 is inserted against it. The activities for the objective are then numbered sequentially 4.1.1, 4.1.2, 4.1.3, and so on. The programme area should be identified clearly in a few words; directional indicators, such as ' increase ' should be omitted. In the OBJECTIVE space a clear concise statement of what the librarian plans to accomplish is inserted.

Against MEASUREMENT METHOD is written a clear statement of how the attainment of the objective is to be measured. The SEQUENCE OF ACTIVITIES lists the specific activities to be taken as steps toward achieving the objectives. The list is designed to assist with planning, and the activities should not be worded so as to form substitute or supplementary objectives. These activities should include provision for review of progress toward the objective. Often this will form one check point for all activities and hence appear as the last

4	PROGRAMME AREA Written communication	
4.1	OBJECTIVE By the beginning of 1974 complete training programme for all staff and institute a) staff news sheet, b) staff manuals, c) annual departmental reports.	Priority 1

MEASUREMENT METHOD

Existence of staff news sheet, staff manuals and departmental reports, and acceptance of their quality by the librarian & deputy. Effectiveness of training programme to be determined according to methods agreed at a senior staff meeting, held at the conclusion of the programme.

SEQUENCE OF ACTIVITIES

		Complete by	Date Com- pleted
4.1.1	Investigation & assessment of need	End of June 1973	
4.1.2	Six hours training for departmental heads	„ July 1973	
4.1.3	Ten hours initial training for other seniors	„ Aug. 1973	
4.1.4	Ten hours initial training for junior staff	„ Aug. 1973	
4.1.5	Assessment of future and continuous training and instruction requirements	„ Sept. 1973	
4.1.6	Institute monthly staff news sheet/magazine, with contributions from all departments	„ Nov. 1973	
4.1.7	Institute departmental staff manuals	„ Jan. 1974	
4.1.8	Institute complete library staff manual	„ April '74	
4.1.9	Institute annual reports from departmental heads to chief librarian	„ April '74	

ACTUAL PERFORMANCE

Fig 5 OBJECTIVE RECORD SHEET

activity on the objective record sheet. If the programme is a lengthy one it may, on the other hand, be desirable to insert more than one review check point in the list of activities.

Dates by which the activity is planned to be completed or started and by which the activity is actually completed or started are inserted in columns by the list of activities. Finally, space is left for a statement of the extent to which the objective, not the programme of activities, was actually achieved, as measured by the measurement method established, in the time set. This statement is obviously compiled after the review or check point and is worded in a similar fashion to the objective so that comparisons can be made. It includes a statement of whether the objective was over-achieved, just achieved or under-achieved, plus an explanation of this level of achievement.

Cost benefit analysis
Before actually embarking on the implementation of a plan it may be thought desirable to obtain some indication of the advantage to the library of taking this action. It is possible to cost library service on the basis of unit cost per issue (*eg* Hamburg) or work necessary to answer an enquiry (*eg* Mason), as a step toward the measurement of effectiveness. A second step would be to provide a basis for evaluation by comparing the figures arrived at with those of a similar library (*ie* having roughly the same number of staff, same work load, etc) or additional sets of figures calculated at future six or twelve month intervals (taking into account rises in costs, such as staff salaries). To measure an aspect of administration such as staff communication is a much more difficult problem, since the investigator encounters intangible costs or benefits like staff morale. Reddin, for example, indicates that ' good relations ' are not measurable except by highly subjective methods and states his maxim : ' If you cannot measure it forget about it because no one will want to know anyway ' (Reddin 75). However, people may not want to know the cost of ' good relations ' simply because they assume that it cannot be measured and hence do not ask. Furthermore, the advice ' forget about it ' (*ie* measurements of effectiveness) is unhelpful if it distracts concern away from intangibles such as good relations or staff morale, since obviously these are factors of vital concern to any library administrator.

An elementary cost benefit analysis of a proposed communica-

184

tion programme could be undertaken as a preliminary to the implementation of the plan. Such an analysis, however imprecise it might be, due to the presence of intangible elements or subjective analysis, would have certain advantages. The analysis would normally consist of work necessary to present the decision taker with the information which he requires to make a decision and to the task of taking the decision itself. Such procedures could be linked to the evaluation of the existing situation and to the preparation of a plan, and provide a focus of interest, definition and appraisal other than general conceptions relating to 'progress made' or 'general advantages of the plan'. Furthermore, the decision taker (*ie* the librarian) might be required or find it advisable to have his decision, in the form of a recommendation relating to implementation, considered by his library committee. In the latter circumstances some sort of costing would be useful for the librarian in his presentation.

A preliminary distinction between 'cost effectiveness' and 'cost benefit analysis' might be helpful before the argument is presented in further detail. In cost effectiveness analysis, effectiveness is viewed in terms of a ratio with cost to form a measurement of efficiency (say of communication). This can be represented diagrammatically as:

$$\text{Efficiency} = \frac{\text{Effectiveness}}{\text{Cost}}$$

To this extent its features accord with those of cost benefit analysis. Cost effectiveness analysis, however, is specifically directed to problems in which outputs (say benefits of a communication programme) cannot be evaluated in market prices but where the inputs can. Such analysis is undertaken to facilitate choice between different systems (*eg* weapons systems) where it is felt that the introduction of one system is necessary and desirable, even though precise results and benefits cannot be measured. Cost benefit analysis, on the other hand, attempts to relate measures of inputs to output, the difference in the two measures being the basic cost benefit which it is felt will result from the introduction of a proposed plan. The benefit could, of course, be a negative one and hence the plan might not be implemented (*eg* if the costs to the community and environment of the building of a new airport exceeded benefits from its establishment).

In line with the above analysis, a cost benefit analysis of a

185

communication plan in a library could focus on a particular aspect of communication, say, transfer of written requests and orders among library departments and branches and hence could include appraisal of more than one system. Consideration could be given to the use of the telephone, telex and portering or messenger systems, as alternatives. On the other hand, a more general cost benefit analysis relating to a communication plan as a whole would be largely considered with one system in mind, measuring the benefits of introducing that system against the benefits or otherwise of not introducing it. Admittedly, some comparison between systems would arise in the sense that considerations relating to the benefit of not introducing a new system would include analysis of the efficiency of the existing one but in terms of introducing a new system only one such system is considered.

A basic problem of analysis is to assign a measure of cost to a system and its performance. Apart from specific or tangible costs such as the cost of paper in written communication, such analysis will be in the form of estimates, conceptual derivations relating to a communication model of the communication system. Ideally, one would like to examine the performance of the system in the real world, as costs would then be easier to calculate. It is unlikely, however, that a librarian will find another library which can be used as an accurate basis for real world measurement and comparison. Such a library would be in a similar state to the one under consideration, would have introduced a successful communication programme and hence be a viable example for analysis and costing. Certainly, elements of a communication system (*eg* a telex system for inter-branch communication) can be analysed in other libraries, in real world situations, but it is highly doubtful whether such conditions would apply to a complete system.

In these circumstances the librarian must revert to a model world in which he creates a model or abstract representation of the real system he proposes to introduce, with which he can manipulate and experiment. The danger with this method is that the model may not be an adequate representation of the real world and conclusions drawn from the model system may prove wrong or inapplicable in practice. This is, of course, a disadvantage of many plans and estimations and is to be accepted if analysis of possible benefits is required. Furthermore, models are useful since their formulation helps clarify and concentrate thinking about the system.

186

A model used in connection with a communication plan should be prescriptive (or normative), as opposed to merely descriptive; it will include conceptual ideals and aims, indicating what ought to be done, rather than presenting a descriptive plan for the librarian to study. To provide information for the solution of real world problems the model should meet three criteria: 1 relevance, 2 feasibility and 3 utility (Howland 507). If relevant it will direct the librarian's attention to the most important areas for consideration and will provide a guide to decision making and implementation. Feasibility implies that the methodological problems encountered can be solved, at least conceptually. Utility implies that the system can be used to design and regulate the final plan.

The quality of any model or abstraction representing the real world depends in large part on the availability and input of good and accurate data. In this respect the quality of a model of an aspect of administration, such as communication, and the relating cost benefit analysis may not be as high as that of a more precise system (say a weapons system), since not all the inputs into the analysis will be controllable in the sense of being amenable to accurate measurement. An important cost, for example, might be the time taken for staff to adjust to a new system, the resultant initial disruption of their work and so on.

As indicated above, however, this is to be accepted in an analysis of a system such as a communication plan. Most limitations will relate to outputs (benefits) but it is necessary to include some estimation of intangibles since in this case the intangibles are objectives. Cost benefit analysis is undertaken primarily to help choose or make a decision on the implementation of a policy or course of action. The latter is a means by which it is hoped the objectives can be attained. Hence some measure of intangible objectives is desirable.

The calculated costs of a communication plan should encompass costs of investigation and drawing up the plan, plus its implementation. These costs can then be set against projected benefits. The benefits considered are usually comparatively short-term benefits, those accruing up to one year after implementation, so as to reduce as much as possible the element of unrealistic speculation involved. G T Vardaman usefully distinguishes between 1 monetary, 2 job and 3 psychological costs and benefits (Vardaman 16-27). Monetary costs are the directly calculable expenses of staff time (man hours) and materials. They would cover the time taken by one or more persons to investigate the problem, the time of other members of staff taken up with discussions and consultation, time taken by the librarian and his senior administrators in examining and assessing the information presented and arriving at a decision, and time involved in presenting the plan to staff (*eg* at staff meetings) and implementing it. Material costs would cover all paper and printing used in such a period on the business at hand.

Job costs relate to actual or potential losses resulting from impaired staff performance during the period of investigation and more significantly during the implementation of the plan. A communication plan will obviously be introduced with the aim of improving efficiency. For example, if departmental heads are provided with more frequent and accurate information and instruction relating to the work of their departments they could perform their own tasks and regulate the work of their staff more easily and effectively. However, a communication plan is bound to result in some disturbance of staff; they will spend time thinking about it and settling down to new methods and routines. A costing of this disturbance will obviously be more subjective than that of monetary costs but could be determined from a consensus of calculations derived from key departmental heads. Considerations of staff time will be included in these calculations but the main element of costing should relate to estimated delays in service or work. Some unit costing of library activities could be brought into these calculations. Thus, if a costing has been made of the work undertaken in answering an average reference enquiry, this could be related to considerations of delay in such service by reference staff adjusting to a communication system and possibly to changes in their routines.

Psychological costs are an even more subjective consideration but they often have a correspondingly important impact. As with job costs, psychological costs (*eg* impact on work and efficiency of mental attitudes resulting from the disturbance of introducing a new system) could be determined from a consensus of the opinion of departmental heads, plus an additional sample of representative receivers. People asked for such estimates could be told to think of a scale of costing, relating to staff time, output and efficiency, in which directly calculable monetary costs would form the basis of comparison for estimates of psychological costs. In making such estimates they should have a clear knowledge of the objectives of the programme, such knowledge providing areas of investigation and calculation for their minds. Further, they should think in terms of expected cost (or expected value when considering psychological benefits) rather than most likely costs (or benefits). The reason for this is that one can easily think about what is most likely to happen, this thought process leading to mere introspection. On the other hand, one cannot guess at expected cost without making more realistic calculations, without going through the process of attributing probabilities to a whole set of possible outcomes.

As indicated in the case of psychological costs, benefits (monetary, job and psychological) are subject to similar calculation processes. An improved communication system could result in the reduction of a flood of ineffective written communications, thus saving materials and staff time preparation. Job benefits would relate to time and work as do job costs.

If the same basis for calculating both costs and benefits is used, errors in, say, subjective judgement should balance out when comparing costs with benefits. This follows even if it is considered that the prediction reliability of monetary costs and benefits falls within the 75 to 100 percent scale and the prediction of psychological costs and benefits within the 25 to 50 percent scale.

The various elements of a cost benefit analysis can be presented in mathematical terms (Frost 200-8). In the present study, analysis has been presented as a series of analytical steps in descriptive form. In either method, however, it is useful to present the results of the analysis in a table, showing costs and benefits. This may be a simple table setting monetary, job and psychological costs against monetary, job and psychological benefits. Such a listing is given in the following example of calculations relating to the establishment of a communication programme in a library with a staff of 70 persons. To some extent the example is hypothetical, although a particular library was considered for the necessary calculations. The costing is a short-range one, in the sense that a period of one year is allocated to the plan (*ie* formulation, implementation and revision). As in all cost benefit analysis, the assumption is made that the library has the necessary resources, people, and control mechanism for undertaking the study and implementing the plan if desired, for adjusting plans to reality and for ensuring that people carry out plans properly.

7

	Costs	Benefits	Total
Monetary	−£5,000	+£2,000	−£3,000
Job	−£2,000	+£4,500	+£2,500
Psychological	−£0,900	+£7,000	+£6,100
TOTAL	−£7,900	+£13,500	+£5,600

Network representation

The plan-making process itself can be plotted, analysed and represented in diagrammatic form by means of a network. An example of such a network has been produced by the Department of the Environment and covers nine main stages, identified as:

1 preparing the programme
2 defining the aims
3 assembling and analysing information
4 forecasting
5 identifying the main policy choices
6 generating and testing alternative strategies
7 preparing the draft plan
8 adjusting the plan to meet representations
9 submitting the plan
(G B Dept of the Environment).

The above stages correspond roughly to those presented in this chapter, from the formulation of objectives to preparation of the plan. However, the representation of a system by a network diagram will here be limited to the plan and the stages of its implementation.

Network analysis involves the representation of the plan under consideration by means of arrows and circles. The arrows represent the 'activities' or jobs to be done during the project and the circles 'events', the points in time at which these activities can start or finish, as the case may be. Each event is allocated a code number. More than one activity can start from or terminate at an event but an activity cannot start until its preceding event has occurred, that is when all activities which terminate at that event have been completed.

A network diagram is constructed to show the logical sequence in which the activities must be performed. It is initially built up to depict the logical sequence of the activities. Time durations are then applied to the activities. In this manner it is possible to determine that sequence of activities through the network which takes the longest (*ie* the critical path, establishing the minimum project duration) and those other paths which are not critical but which have spare time or 'float' available to them. With the critical path established it is then possible to reconsider the other paths or activities, the resources available and the relative timings involved, so as to depict the most logical and seemingly best sequence of events.

The steps outlined so far will be facilitated by the planner asking himself questions such as:

1 what activities have to be done
2 how broad or detailed should the activities be
3 in what order must they be done (which must precede which; which activities may be concurrent)
4 how long will they take to do
5 which must be completed by particular dates
6 what resources (staff time, materials, etc) will be available.

It is quite often difficult to show exact relationships or directions and it is not always possible to define results of activities. Nevertheless, this does not detract from the value of network analysis. Not only is it an aid to planning, but it also indicates ways of obtaining better control of a project during its implementation. Hence the structure must be flexible to accommodate such development, additions and changes as may seem to be desirable. Alternative courses of action should always be considered. Such a process is linked to evaluation of the project progress and results.

In the initial stages of plan formulation, where details are obscure, an initial skeleton network may be produced, indicating the main guide lines for action only. Individual departments or persons could then be required to formulate more detailed sequences of activities relating to their own work, to fit into the general framework. The final network for a communication system (*ie* an administrative element) will be less detailed than that for, say, constructing a factory, where day-to-day control is necessary. The main purpose of the network representation, the communication plan and its implementation, will be to give a broad overall picture of the project, although obviously more detail will be evident than in the initial skeleton network. The final network may comprise a number of sectional networks relating to departments. Since communication problems are common to all departments, however, it would be more practicable to have a series of sectional networks arranged according to technical or functional areas rather than

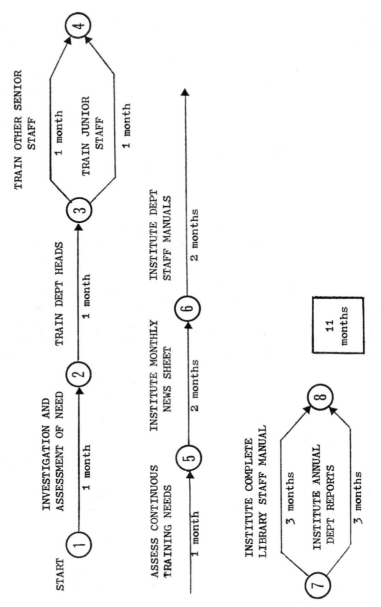

Fig 6 WRITTEN COMMUNICATION. OBJECTIVE: BY THE END OF 1974
COMPLETE TRAINING PROGRAMME FOR ALL STAFF AND INSTITUTE
(A) STAFF NEWS SHEET, (B) STAFF MANUALS, (C) ANNUAL DEPART-
MENTAL REPORTS

departmental or geographic considerations. An example could be that of written communication, given earlier in this chapter.

It will be seen from figure 6 that in two cases activities run concurrently: *Train other senior staff/train junior staff,* and *Institute complete library staff manual/institute annual departmental reports.* It might be thought that other activities could run concurrently, namely *Institute monthly news sheet* and *Institute departmental staff manuals.* Admittedly, the start of one is not logically dependent upon the completion of the other, but it is necessary to take into account senior staff time to deal with these activities and hence the completion of one is specified as a preliminary to the start of the other. As a final embellishment, times can be added to the network. It will be seen that individual stages take from one to three months to complete and the complete operation is phased over an eleven month period, that is eleven months is the earliest event time by which the sequence will be completed.

Such sectional networks, modified where necessary, may be combined to present an overall view of the plan and its implementation. It is usual to divide such a presentation by horizontal zones, in this case each zone representing a particular type of communication or activity. The diagram can further be divided vertically by columns representing time sequences to save writing all the time sequences onto the network itself. The network example given in this chapter relates to the institution of communication elements (*eg* departmental staff manuals).

The division of the network into time periods (the cycle of events being phased over a twelve month period), as well as the arrangement of the network in the traditional manner (a sequence going from left to right), gives an indication of the sequence of events. If it is desired to number the events more specifically, parallel horizontal events can be given a common number (as in the network presented in this chapter) or linked by dummy arrows. A dummy arrow requires neither time nor resources but can show that certain events are in sequence. Hence a section of the network could be represented thus:

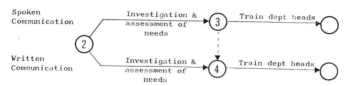

The dummy arrow indicates that, due, say, to limited resources of staff time, the training of departmental heads in written communication has to await the investigation and assessment of needs of both oral and written communication. The training of departmental heads in oral communication can proceed as soon as the investigation and assessment of needs of oral communication has been accomplished but does not, of course, have to wait for the investigation and assessment of needs of written communication. In a network such as the one presented, however, the introduction of a number of these dummies at the planning stage could complicate the whole picture. Such dummies could be introduced at later dates if it was necessary to separate activities due to lack of resources for their concurrent enactment. This is possible since, as indicated earlier, the plan should be kept under constant review during its implementation and not merely during an activity such as 'assessment of continuous training needs' specifically provided in the network. Progress can be indicated on the network by means of coloured markers (supplemented by a written record in the form of objective record sheets detailed above), while changes in the plan can be recorded on both the network diagrams and the relevant objective record sheets.

Implementation

Implementation of any plan will involve the adjustment of staff duties and responsibilities, plus alterations in staff relationships. Hence it can be seen that a plan impinges on sensitive areas of staff administration and it must be appreciated that care and caution are required during this part of the programme. If the plan has been formulated with the assistance of a working group, this planning team can now facilitate the implementation by coordinating departmental instruction and so on. Whether such a team exists or not, staff must be given adequate warning as to the implementation dates and objectives, plus full information relevant to their activities on content and progress. Employee participation in the formulation of the plan is to be encouraged; a similar participation of all staff, not merely of members of a planning team, should be sought during implementation. This can be obtained by periodic staff meetings at which comments and suggestions are seen to be welcomed from all members of staff. If such facilities are provided, control—the administrative mechanism for ensuring that people carry out the plan—will be easier to operate.

Evaluation and revision

Any plan, once implemented, may display inadequacies because it was conceived with only ideals or models of the real world in mind, rather than in actual situations. Furthermore, new directions, new possibilities, may become evident to the planner as implementation proceeds. Such new directions or possibilities do not necessarily reveal deficiencies in the original plan but can, alternatively, be seen as added improvements of a basically sound plan. To accommodate changes of either category the plan must be flexible. Staff participation, as discussed under the heading of *Implementation,* can help reveal difficulties in the plan, indicate new directions and facilitate plan amendments as well.

So that close control can be maintained it is necessary to measure actual progress, compare this with maintained progress, guage the effect of any deviation from the plan, and replan to meet new circumstances. This should be a continuous process during the implementation of the plan. The frequency of the review will depend on the amount of control required and the amount of detail contained in the plan. In the case of a library communication plan it should prove sufficient to update the schedule every month. Progress is then measured by recording the actual time taken to complete each activity and if necessary reassessing the duration of activities in progress or those still to be implemented.

At the end of plan, implementation—progress made in the whole series of activities—should be reviewed to evaluate the effectiveness of the programme. Such evaluation may be recorded on the objective record sheets, supplemented by a general report and should be subject to staff discussion in a similar manner to which formulation of objectives and plan were achieved. It may be necessary to consider the formation of additional plans to implement activities whose success has, in the implementation of the original plan, been of a dubious nature and to facilitate implementation of further elements whose presence or desirability has only recently been revealed. Such additional plans will be of smaller scale than the original one. However, attention devoted to communication and the related administrative fields such as staff training should not diminish in a like manner once the original programme has finished. The aim should be to keep the communication gain derived from the programmes as well as effecting continuous improvement and revision of communication standards and objectives. Communication

Fig 7 NETWORK REPRESENTATION OF A LIBRARY COMMUNICATION PLAN AND ITS IMPLEMENTATION

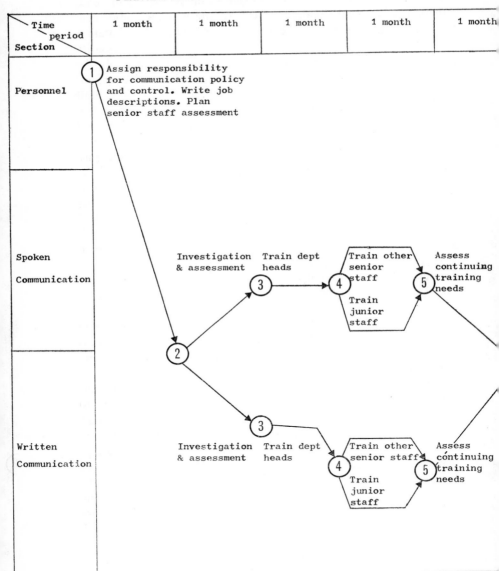

month	1 month	1 month	1 month	1 month	1 month

stitute
aff meetings
r whole lib

Institute
meetings for
dept heads

stitute
aff meetings
r senior staff

Institute
junior
staff
meetings

⑧   ⑨

Institute
counselling procedures

Institute
visits to
outlying
libraries

⑩

Institute
appraisal
interviews

stitute monthly
ws sheet

stitute
nos

ke lib
nt minutes
ailable
staff

⑦

Institute dept
staff manuals

Institute
monthly dept
reports

⑨

Institute complete
lib staff manual

Institute annual
dept reports

⑪

Copy of
library's
annual
report
to all
staff

⑫

7*

is a continuous process, so should be its study and control in any library.

The communication programme should help identify areas for future development and improvement. So far as more immediate benefits are concerned, such a programme should aid total library effectiveness in a number of ways. It should facilitate the better coordination of the library by clarifying areas of responsibility and individual contributions and importances, helping to eliminate duplication of effort and conflict. Certain improved individual performances should result from the more adequate instruction and supply of information, plus clearer definition of individual responsibilities and roles. Both improvements may well help to boost staff morale and heightened effort in library services.

Any organisation is subject to processes of continuous, if gradual, change. If library administrators pay attention to staff communication—an integral part of administrative techiques and processes—then it is likely that they will be aware of changes, such as the effect of new library services on the administrative structure and staff relationships, that take place and attempt to condition or, indeed, effect changes in a constructive manner. The actions of library administrators will be constructive if they seek to ensure staff acceptance of changes that are necessary in order to improve library services in the light of the developing requirements of a particular library's clientele.

Not all changes, of course, have significance for the library as a whole or require months of deliberate planning. Many changes occur on a day-to-day basis, yet may prove to be more irksome to staff and provoke more resistance than wholesale library-wide changes such as amalgamation or automation, which are often accorded high levels of corrective attention by administrators. Joan Woodward's team of investigators found that most of the organisational changes in the industries they studied were not deliberately planned. They had come about almost spontaneously, as a result of a crisis, to accommodate individuals or in response to a management fashion (Woodward 192).

Any change is accomplished through persons, the human element of an organisation. As Keith Davis has pointed out, organisational change does not produce a direct adjustment as in the case of air molecules but, instead, it operates through employee's attitudes to produce a response conditioned by his feelings toward the change

(Davis, 1957 140). A classic series of experiments conducted by Roethlisberger and his associates showed that there is no necessarily direct connection between the change and the responses (Roethlisberger; Roethlisberger & Dickson). Each changed situation is interpreted by the individual according to his attitudes. The way he feels about the change determines how he will respond to it. Attitudes themselves are caused by such individual aspects as personal history and background, social experiences, outside work and the work environment itself with its pattern of staff links and relationships. To attempt to create favourable attitudes toward change it is necessary for the librarian to remove staff fears relating to, say, undesirable increase in workloads; to help staff understand the change, its purpose, content and probable results; and to encourage them to think in new ways, to approach new situations with new frames of mind.

One difficulty facing the librarian in such efforts is that activities which help get change accepted, such as effective communication, are themselves often disrupted by change. Since, from this point of view, such stabilising processes as communication may be weakest at the time they are most needed, senior staff need to make special efforts to maintain them at high levels of effectiveness during periods of change. Since, however, some changes occur daily, the foregoing statement implies continuous attention to staff communication and its effectiveness. The advantage of investigating communication in a library or of a communication programme is that it involves the study and amendment of the organisational structure, staff positions and training programme. By seeking improvement in these areas and the maintenance of communication channels and processes that will not crumble under pressure, library management should be able to influence human behaviour and attitudes in an indirect manner and ensure more efficient achievement of library goals.

Bibliography

Abell, M D 'Aspects of upward communications in a public library' In: M L Bundy & R Aronsen, *eds Social and political aspects of librarianship: student contributions to library science* Albany: State University of New York at Albany, School of Librarianship, 1965 91-9.

Allen, L A *The management profession* NY: McGraw-Hill, 1964.

Allen, T J & Cohen, S I 'Information flow in research and development laboratories' *Adm Sci Quart,* 14 (1) March 1969 12-19.

American Library Association *Library Administration Division. Personnel services rating report* Rev ed Chicago: ALA, 1970.

Argyle, M *Social Interaction* London: Methuen, 1969.

Armstrong-Wright, A T *Critical path method: introduction and practice* London: Longmans, 1969.

Ashworth, W 'The administration of diffuse collections' *Aslib Proc,* 24 (5) May 1972 274-83.

Association of Research Libraries *Problems in university library management* Wash, DC: ARL, 1970.

BACIE *Report writing* 2nd ed London: BACIE, 1961.

BACIE *Tips on talking* 2nd ed London: BACIE, 1960.

Bales, R F 'In conference' *Harvard Busin R,* 32 (2) March-April 1954 44-50.

Barnard, C *The functions of the executive* Cambridge, Ma: Harvard UP, 1938.

Bartlett, F C *The mind at work and play* London: Allen & Unwin, 1951.

Bass, B M *Leadership, psychology and organizational behavior* NY: Harper, 1960.

Bassnett, P J *Spatial and administrative relationships in large public libraries.* FLA Thesis, 1971.

Berkowitz, R L 'Personnel evaluation' *Law Libr J,* 65 (2) May 1972 154-7.

Berloo, D K *The process of communication: an introduction to theory and practice* NY: Holt, Rinehart & Winston, 1960.

Berne, E 'Concerning the nature of communication' *Psychiat Q,* 27 1953 185-98.

Birmingham Corporation *Forward: a handbook for junior entrants* 1961.

Birmingham Public Libraries *Staff handbook* nd.

Blau, P M & Scott, W R *Formal organizations* London: Routledge & KP, 1963.

Blum, G S 'An experimental reunion of psychoanalytical theory with perceptual vigilance and defense' *J abnorm soc Psychol,* 49 1954 94-8.

Blumstein, A 'The choice of analytical techniques' In: Washington Operations Research Council *Cost effectiveness analysis: new approaches in decision-making* Ed T A Goldman NY: Praeger, 1967 33-43.

Brewer, J 'Flow of communications, expert qualifications and organizational authority structures' *Amer Sociol R,* 36 (3) June 1971 475-84.

British Institute of Management *Communication: a study of employee information in twelve companies* London: BIM, 1958.

Brown, J A C *The social psychology of industry* Harmondsworth, Middx: Penguin Books, 1954.

Brown, W B P *Explorations in management* London: Heinemann, 1960.

Bryant, D W 'Centralization and decentralization at Harvard' *Coll Res Libr,* 22 (5) Sept 1961 328-34.

Burns, T *Management in the electronics industry: a study of eight English companies* University of Edinburgh, Social Science Research Centre, 1958.

Burns, T & Stalker, G M *The management of innovation* London: Tavistock, 1961.

Chapple, R T & Read, W L *A textbook of human communications* London: Macdonald & Evans, 1963.

Cherry, E C *On human communication: a review, a survey and a criticism* 2nd ed Cambridge, Ma: MIT Press, 1966.

City of Leeds *Town Clerk's Office. Management Services & Establishment Division. Training Section. Leeds City Libraries: Library Assistants training programme* nd.

Cook, P H 'An examination of the notion of communication in industry ' *Occup Psychol,* 25 (1) Jan 1951 1-14.

Dale, E & Urwick, L F *Staff in organization* NY : McGraw-Hill, 1960.

Dance, F E X ' Toward a theory of human communication ' In : F E X Dance, *ed Human communication theory: original essays* NY : Holt, Rinehart & Winston, 1967 288-309.

Davis, K *Human relations in business* NY : McGraw-Hill, 1957.

Davis, K ' Making constructive use of the office grapevine ' In : American Management Association *New dimensions in office management* NY : AMA, 1942 25-35.

Davis, K ' Management communication and the grapevine ' *Harvard Busin R,* 31 (5) Sept-Oct 1953 43-9.

Davis, K 'A method of studying communication patterns in organizations ' *Personn Psychol,* 6 (3) Autumn 1953 301-12.

Dean, J R ' Senior staff training: an approach ' *Libr Wld,* 70 (828) June 1969 339-41.

DeProspero, E ' Personnel evaluation as an impetus to growth ' *Libr trends,* 20 (1) July 1971, 60-70.

Detroit Public Library *Your job with Detroit Public Library: a handbook for employees* 1959.

Dorsey, J T 'A communication model for administration ' *Adm Sci Quart,* 2 Dec 1957 307-24.

Dudley County Borough *Libraries, Museums & Arts Department. An introduction* nd.

Dudley Public Library Private communication from J Hoyle, Librarian, March 1972.

Durham County Library *A manual for new members of staff* 1969.

Eilon, S *Management control* London : Macmillan, 1971.

Enoch Pratt Free Library *Staff instruction book. Section C. Staff relationships* 1965 ed.

Etzioni, A 'Authority, structure and organizational effectiveness ' *Adm Sci Quart,* 4 (1) Jan 1959 43-67.

Etzioni, A *A comparative analysis of complex organizations* NY : Free Press, 1961.

Exeter University Library Private communication from C F Scott, Deputy Librarian, Feb 1972.

Fayol, H *General and industrial management* Trans by C Storrs London : Pitman, 1946.

Forgotson, J 'Communication in the library' *Wilson Libr Bull,* 24 (6) Feb 1960 427-8.

Frost, M J *Values for money: the technique of cost benefit analysis* London: Gower Press, 1971.

Garnett, J *The manager's responsibility for communication* London: The Industrial Society, 1971.

Gibbs, C B & Brown, I D 'Increased production from the information incentive in a representative task' *Manager,* 24 (5) May 1956 374-9.

Glamorgan County Library *Staff manual for part time branch librarians* 1968.

Gloucestershire County Library *Staff code* 6th ed 1970.

Grace, H A 'Confidence, redundancy and the purpose of communication' *J Communication,* 6 (1) Spring 1956, 16-23.

GB *Civil Service Department. Job appraisal review training manual* London: HMSO, 1971.

GB *Department of the Environment. Management networks: a study for structure plans* London: HMSO, 1971.

GB *Department of the Environment. Directorate of Building Development. The planned open office: a primer for management* London: HMSO, 1971.

Gscheidle, G E 'Departments in public libraries' *Libr Trends,* 7 (3) Jan 1959 437-47.

Guetzkow, H & Simon, H A 'The impact of certain communication nets upon organization and performance in task-oriented groups' *Manag Sci,* 1 (3-4) April-July 1955 233-50.

Gunning, R *The technique of clear writing* NY: McGraw-Hill, 1952.

Hamburg, M & others 'Library objectives and performance measures—their use in decision making' *Libr Q,* 42 (1) Jan 1972 107-28.

Henderson, F 'What's being done?' In: *New directions in staff development: moving from ideas to actions. Papers of a one day conference held in Detroit, Michigan, 28 June 1970* Ed E W Stone Chicago: ALA, Admin Div, 1971 11-15.

Hepworth, J B 'Communications and library management' *Libr Wld,* 67 (797) May 1966 324-9.

Higham, T M 'Basic psychological factors in communication' *Occup Psychol,* 31 (1) Jan 1957 1-10.

Hoslett, S D 'Barriers to communication' *Personnel,* 28 Sept 1951 108-14.

Howland, D 'A regulatory model for system design and operation' In: J R Lawrence, *ed Operational research and the social sciences* London: Tavistock, 1966 505-15.

' INTAMEL: review of the three year research and exchange programme approved at the 4th annual meeting in Baltimore in 1971 ' *Int Lib. Rev,* 4 (2) April 1972 251-62.

Irving, A *Improving industrial communication* London: Industrial Society, 1970.

Jackson, J M ' The organization and its communication problems ' *J Communication,* 9 (4) Dec 1959 158-67.

Jennings, H H *Leadership and isolation* 2nd ed London: Longmans, 1950.

Jones, K ' Staff deployment ' *Libr Wld,* 73 (864) June 1972 320-3.

Karlins, M & Abelson, H I *Persuasion: how opinions and attitudes are changed* 2nd ed London: Lockwood, 1970.

Kelly, H H ' Communication in experimentally created hierarchies ' *Hum Relat,* 4 (1) Feb 1951, 39-56.

Lamb, W ' To make a gesture ' *20th Cent,* 177 (1037) 1968 30-3.

Lanark County Library *Staff manual* nd.

Lawrence, R P ' How to deal with resistance to change ' *Harvard Busin R,* 32 (3) May-June 1954, 49-57.

Leicestershire County Library *A manual of working instructions: an algorithm outline of clerical work routines and procedures* Preliminary working copy 1970.

Library of Congress Details of the Human Relations Committees and Council are given in: *Libr of Congress Info Bull,* 31 (27) July 7 1972 A-108; 31 (31) Aug 4 1972 347-9; 31 (34) Aug 25 1972 383-4.

Likert, R 'A motivational approach to the modified theory of organization and management' In: M Haire, *ed Modern organization theory* NY: Wiley, 1959 184-217.

Likert, R *New patterns of management* NY: McGraw-Hill, 1961.

Little, P *Communication in business* London: Longmans, 1965.

McAnally, A M ' Departments in university libraries ' *Libr Trends,* 7 (3) Jan 1959, 448-64.

McColvin, L R ' The function of the public library ' *Libr Ass Rec,* 54 (5) May 1952 158-61.

McCormack J S 'Communication and the organization' *Adv Mgmt J*, 33 (1) Jan 1968, 63-7.

McDiarmid, E W & McDiarmid, J *The administration of the American public library* Chicago: ALA, 1943.

McDonald, J P 'Rutgers University Library: a study of current problems of organization and service in a decentralized library' In: *Studies in library administration directed by Keyes D Metcalf* New Brunswick: Rutgers UP, 1960 95-132.

McGreal, R 'In-service training at the Library of New South Wales' In: J Ponder, *ed Management in libraries* Melbourne: Ormond, 1971 46-60.

McGregor, D 'The human side of enterprise' In: *Proceedings of the fifth anniversary convocation of the School of Industrial Management, Massachusetts Institute of Technology, Cambridge, Ma, 1957.* Also published under the same title as: *The human side of enterprise* NY: McGraw-Hill, 1960.

McGregor, D 'An uneasy look at performance and appraisal' *Harvard Busin R,* 35 (3) May-June 1957 89-94.

McLuhan, M *Understanding the media: the extensions of man* NY: McGraw-Hill, 1964.

Maier, N R F *Principles of human relations: applications to management* London: Chapman & Hall, 1952.

Maslow, A *Motivation and personality* NY: Harper & Row, 1954.

Mason, D 'PPBS: application to an industrial information and reference service' *J Librarianship,* 4 (2) April 1972, 91-105.

Meerloo, J A M 'Contributions of psychiatry to the study of communication' In: F E X Dance, *ed Human communication theory: original essays* NY: Holt, Rinehart & Winston, 1967 130-59.

Metcalf, K D *Report on the Harvard University Library: a study of present and prospective problems* Cambridge, Ma: Harvard Univ Lib, 1955.

Moonman, E *Communication in an expanding organization: a case study in action research* London: Tavistock, 1970.

Moreno, J L *Who shall survive: a new approach to the problem of human relationships* NY: Beacon House, 1934.

Morgan, J S *Getting across to employees: a guide to effective communication on the job* NY: McGraw-Hill, 1964.

Newcomb, R & Sammons, M 'Communication clinic' *Personnel,* 37 (1) Jan-Feb 1960 76-80.

New York Public Library *A handbook for new staff members* 1954.

Nichols, R G & Stevens, L A 'Listening to people' *Harvard Busin R,* 35 (5) Sept-Oct 1957 85-92.

Northway, M L *A primer of sociometry* 2nd ed Univ of Toronto Press, 1967.

Ogden, C K & Richards, F A *The meaning of meaning* NY : Harcourt, Brace & Co, 1923.

Oliver, R T 'Contributions of the speech profession to the study of human communication' In : F E X Dance, *ed Human communication theory: original essays* NY : Holt, Rinehart & Winston, 1967 264-87.

Openheinm, A N *Questionnaire design and attitude measurement* London : Heinemann, 1966.

Ottemiller, J H 'The management engineer' *Libr Trends,* 2 (3) Jan 1954 437-51.

Paerdee, J 'The special requirements of the larger unit in personnel administration' *Libr Trends,* 13 (3) Jan 1965 353-63.

Peele, D 'Some aspects of staff evaluation in the UK and the USA' *Libr Ass Rec,* 74 (4) April 1972 69-71.

Pelz, D C & Andrews, F M *Scientists in organizations: productive climates for research and development* NY : Wiley, 1966.

Perrow, C *Organizational analysis: a sociological view* London : Tavistock, 1970.

Peterson, K G *The University of California Library at Berkeley, 1900-1945* Berkeley : Univ of California Press, 1970.

Plate, K H *Management personnel in libraries: a theoretical model for analysis* Rockaway, NJ : American Faculty Press, 1970.

Platt, J H 'What do we mean—" communication "?' *J Communication,* 5 (1) Spring 1955 21-6.

Prethus, R *Organizational society* NY : Vintage Press, 1962.

Reading University Library *Notes for the staff* July 1970.

Reddin, W J *Effective MBO* London : Management Publications, 1971.

Redfield, C E *Communication in management* Chicago : Univ of Chicago Press, 1958.

Reeves, F W 'Some general principles of administrative organization' In : C B Joeckel, *ed Current issues in library administration* Chicago : Univ of Chicago Press, 1939 1-21.

Rodger, A *The seven point plan* 3rd ed London : NIIP, 1970.

Roethlisberger, F J *Management and morals* Cambridge, Ma : Harvard UP, 1941.

Roethlisberger, F J & Dickson, W J *Management and the worker* Cambridge, Ma : Harvard UP, 1939.

Rowe, K H 'An appraisal of appraisals' *J Manag Stud,* 1 (1) March 1964 1-25.

Rubenstein, A H & Haberstroh, C J, *eds Some theories of organization* Rev ed Homewood, Il : Irwin, 1966.

Ryan, D L 'Libraries in off-campus units' *Libr Trends,* 10 (4) April 1962 541-51.

Saltonstall, R 'What employees want from their work' *Harvard Busin R,* 31 (6) Nov-Dec 1953 72-8.

Schulz, J V von & Kepple, R R 'Library staff newsletter : an experiment in communication' *Spec Libr,* 62 (3) March 1971 151-2.

Shannon, C & Weaver, W *The mathematical theory of communication* Urbana, Il : Univ of Illinois Press, 1949.

Sidney, E & Brown, M *The skills of interviewing* London : Tavistock, 1961.

Siegel, L *Industrial psychology* Rev ed Homewood, Il : Irwin, 1964.

Simon, B V 'The need for administrative know-how in libraries' *Bull Med Libr Assoc,* 57 (2) April 1969 160-70.

Smith, P B 'Training and developing executives' In : D Pym, *ed Industrial society: social sciences in management* Harmondsworth, Middx : Penguin Books, 1968 274-93.

Staffordshire County Library *The new assistant* nd.

Staffordshire County Library *Staff manual* nd.

Starbuck, W H 'Organizational growth and development' In : J E March, *ed A handbook of organizations* Chicago : Rand McNally, 1965 451-533.

Starr, M. K. *Management: a modern approach* NY : Harcourt, Brace, Jovanovich, 1971.

Surrey County Council *Education Committee. County Library. Scheme for trainee librarians* Aug 1971.

Thayer, L O *Communication and communication systems in organization, management and interpersonal relations* Homewood, Il : Irwin, 1968.

Thayer, L O 'On theory building in communication : some conceptual problems' *J Communication,* 13 (4) Dec 1963, 217-35.

Thomas, P A & Ward, V A *Where the time goes* London : Aslib, 1973.

Thompson, V A 'The organizational dimension' *Wilson Libr Bull,* 42 (7) March 1968 693-700.

Townsend, L A 'A corporate president's view of the internal communication function' *J Communication,* 15 (4) Dec 1965 208-15.

'Training programs at LC' *Libr of Congress Info Bull,* 31 (14) April 7 1972 and 31 (15) April 14 1972.

Van Dersal, W R *The successful supervisor in government and business* Rev ed London : Pitman, 1970.

Van Gelder, R *Induction* London : Industrial Society, 1967.

Vardaman, G T *Effective communication of ideas* NY : Van Nostrand-Reinhold, 1970.

Vardaman, G T & Hatterman, C C *Management control through communication: systems for organizational diagnosis and design* NY : Wiley, 1968.

Varley, D H 'The importance of communication' *Liverpool University Libraries Staff Newsletter. New Series,* No 1 Jan 1972 1.

Webber, R A 'Perceptions of interactions between supervisors and subordinates' *Hum Relat,* 23 (3) June 1970 235-48.

Weinshall, T D 'The communicogram: a method for describing the pattern, frequency and accuracy of organization and communication' In : J R Lawrence, *ed Operational research and the social sciences* London : Tavistock, 1966 619-33.

Wheeler, J L & Goldhor, H *Practical administration of public libraries* NY : Harper & Row, 1962.

Wiltshire County Library *Instruction book for assistants in regional and branch libraries* Rev ed 1968.

Woodward, J *Industrial organization: theory and practice* London : OUP, 1965.

Zalenzik, A *Human dilemmas of leadership* NY : Harper, 1966.

Zelko, H P 'An outline of the value of listening in communication' *J Communication,* 4 (3) Fall 1954 71-5.

Index

210